# a place apart

## Houses of Prayer
## & Retreat Centers
## In North America

Compiled by

## Janet Joy

The publisher is very grateful for permission to use the artwork of
the Carmelite Sisters of Flemington, New Jersey. Notecards of many of
the drawings in this book may be ordered by writing to:

ST. TERESA'S PRESS  P.O. Box 785, Flemington  NJ 08822.

Library of Congress Cataloging-in-Publication Data

Joy, Janet, 1938–
      A place apart : houses of prayer & retreat centers in North
America / compiled by Janet Joy.
        p. cm.
    Includes bibliographical references and index.
    ISBN 0-940147-30-0
    1. Houses of prayer--North America--Directories.   2. Retreats-
-North America--Directories.   3. Monasteries--North America--
Guest accommodations.   I Title.
    BX2438.5.J68    1994
    291.6'5'0257--dc20                                    94-42225
                                                              CIP

ISBN: 0-940147-30-0


Source Books
P.O. Box 794
Trabuco Canyon CA 92678

Printed & Bound in the U.S.A by K.N.I., Anaheim  CA.

*This book is dedicated to my Mother*
*for her constant love and support over the years,*
*and for her example of a steadfast and loving Christian.*
*Her simple, undaunted faith and daily Walk with Jesus,*
*through good times and bad, has been her strength*
*and an inspiration to me.*

Let us be praises of the Holy Trinity.

# CONTENTS

# INTRODUCTION

My ministry, A Place Apart, was born from a desire to find information about Houses of Prayer around the world, and to pass it on to people who wish to join in the age-old tradition of pilgrimage as they journey homeward. There are others who search—for what, they know not! But if one is open to spending time in a place apart, a seed might be planted, eyes and ears may be opened to the Truth: to Our Lord and Saviour, Jesus Christ.

Over the last few years I have become convinced of the need for all of us to get away to a quiet place, a retreat experience, whether at a traditional retreat house, a monastery, a hermitage in the wilderness, a cabin in the woods or on the shore, or even quiet time spent in our own place apart that we have created at home.

We are bombarded daily with new information, deadlines, increased responsibilities at home and at work. And we have felt the tragedies of life's litany of losses: the death of a loved one, broken marriages and homes, illness, financial woes, wars and natural disasters. The ability to cope with the complexity and pace of today's world is strained, and sometimes breaks down.

It is important for us to take the time to be quiet, to simplify our lives, rest our minds, and open our hearts to allow God to touch us. With divine guidance we can stay on track as we travel through life. The need for holistic healing is of utmost importance: we must attend to our spiritual well-being as well as to the health of our minds and bodies. Psalm 46 instructs us: *Be still and acknowledge that I am God.* Opportunities abound to fulfill this command as one takes up the spiritual adventure, finding and resting in quiet places.

A few years ago, I began collecting information on retreat centers and houses of prayer from many countries and several Christian traditions, and passing this information on to correspondents. The response has been heartwarming, and has energized me to collect information in great detail. Now it is clear that in book form, a compilation will reach many more pilgrims, and inform them of the great variety of special places which open their doors in peace, love and reconciliation.

I continue to gather and update information from other parts of the world. As my Silent Partner continues to guide me in this labor of love, I pray for health and strength to see this project to completion.

I extend heartfelt thanks to my family and friends for their love, their encouragement and their valuable advice.

May this work be a blessing, not only for me, but also for my loved ones and for those pilgrims who are open to trying another road in pursuit of true peace of mind.

May the Peace, the Joy, and the Love of Christ be with you now and forever.

Janet L. Joy
Fall, 1994

# HOW TO USE THIS BOOK

You know best your criteria for selecting a place to be apart. Perhaps distance is a concern, or wheelchair access, or the availability of a spiritual director, and so on. For the most part this guide gives information authorized by the Retreat Centers and Houses of Prayer themselves, often in great detail, and up-to-date as we go to press. But it must be emphasized that any book such as this has its limitations. Things change.

So it is important that you plan ahead. Some houses of hospitality are fully booked months in advance. When you have found the place you are looking for in this guide, write and ask that a space be reserved for you, giving alternate dates if possible. And if a deposit is required, send it too. Given the nature of many of the monasteries and convents and hermitages in this book, it is often better to write to them than to telephone. If you cannot show up on the given date, let the guest-master know as soon as possible. You will see that some of the places in this book do not accommodate overnight visitors. For these you will have to make separate arrangements.

The individual entries have been arranged by state and province. Several listings are given towards the end of the book under their country heading. There is also an index of the houses of prayer at the back of the book.

As far as possible, the information is given as the individual houses and centers want it presented. Thus the scheme of each entry varies. Take care in reading the whole entry before enquiring. Some retreat centers have provided local sketch-maps. Usually these are not to scale, but are useful for general orientation.

If you are not conversant with the practices and routines of retreat houses and monasteries, you may wish to refer to the *Notes on Terminology* on the following pages. This glossary is not intended to be theologically exhaustive or contentious.

And since spiritual reading is often an integral part of a retreat, at the back of the book there is a booklist which you may find helpful.

# NOTES ON TERMINOLOGY

**ABBESS**  Reverend Mother of a group of contemplative nuns in charge of the community at an abbey. She is elected by the nuns in Chapter (a general meeting) and historically exercises the authority of a bishop within the abbey and any affiliated foundations such as Priories.

**ABBOT**  The male equivalent in a monastery of monks.

**BASILICA**  A church of honor shared by Catholics throughout the world. A place of great faith and devotion and a destination of pilgrims. There are 31 basilicas in the United States.

**BLESSED SACRAMENT**  The consecrated host, the true presence of Our Lord and Savior in the form of bread or unleavened wafer. A Divine Mystery, the Eucharist, given to us at the Last Supper.

**CELL**  The private space of each sister or monk. A humble room, simply furnished, where one communes with God, according to one's own spiritual needs. The Bible usually has a place of honor in this private oratory of prayer, study, work and rest.

**CHAPEL**  A small house or room set aside for prayer, an oratory, found in most retreat houses and monasteries. Monasteries usually have a larger church as well. A chapel lends itself to private prayer and adoration.

**CLOISTER**  An area within the monastic enclosure which is off-limits to laity.

**CLOISTERED NUN**  A woman religious choosing the ancient privilege of making a total commitment, in a formal way, to God—solemn vows of religion. These vows carry an obligation of strict papal enclosure and official recitation of the Divine Office in choir. Called 'Nuns' rather than Sisters.

**CONTEMPLATIO**  A yearning for a closer relationship with God.

**CONTEMPLATIVE**  One who engages in a life of prayer: daily Mass, the Divine Office, spiritual reading, work and study, in a community of men or women. Every action is focussed on the praise and glory of God. A simple and humble lifestyle, most of the time spent in silence. Many seek to share their prayer life with others in simple, informal ways.

**CONVENT**  Home of a group of nuns, usually of one order or congregation, affiliated with a liturgical Christian faith. They live in community, share the workload and usually take vows of poverty, chastity and obedience. The sisters may or may not dress in traditional habit.

**DAY OF RECOLLECTION**  Usually a room is made available to the person seeking time alone to pray, relax, work quietly. Also for groups who attend a day program organized either by the house of prayer or themselves.

**DIRECTED RETREAT – GUIDED RETREAT**  The retreatant meets daily with a spiritual director for personal guidance in prayer and for spiritual counselling. Usually there are tapes, books and leaflets available for one's own use. As with other retreats, the retreatant is invited to join the community in its daily rhythm of prayer.

## DIVINE OFFICE – DAILY OFFICE – LITURGY OF THE HOURS

A rhythm of daily prayer, consisting largely of the Psalms said and/or chanted at specific times of the day in  praise and worship of God. The monastic tradition is to ring a bell to call to mind the various prayer times.

| | |
|---|---|
| VIGILS | The night prayer of the Church, usually prayed in the early morning before the coming of light. |
| LAUDS | Prayer before dawn. |
| PRIME | Prayer at dawn. |
| TERCE | A brief period of prayer in the morning before receiving the Holy Eucharist. |
| SEXT | A brief prayer time at noon. |
| NONE | A brief prayer time in mid-afternoon. |
| VESPERS | Evening prayer, around 6 PM. |
| COMPLINE | Final Office, prayer of the day. The monastic day closes with this prayer time, after which silence falls over the monastery, promoting rest and contemplation of God's Word in the monk's hearts throughout the night. |

**EVENING OF RECOLLECTION**  For groups using retreat house facilities for a program in keeping with the mission of the house.

**EXPOSITION OF THE BLESSED SACRAMENT**  Seen through a window in the center of a monstrance, the Eucharistic host which the faithful adore, while meditating on the Sacred Mystery.  A feeling for mysticism is helpful in appreciating the significance of this gift from Our Lord.

**GREGORIAN CHANT**  Praying the Psalms in song derived from ancient plainchant, unaccompanied by musical instruments. The Chant was developed during the time of Pope Gregory I, and is regularly used in monastic communities during the Divine Office and sometimes the Mass.

**GROUP RETREAT**  A group reserves a certain time for a program at a retreat house, or sometimes brings its own program. Silence prevails when the group is not in session. There is a wide variety of presenters and topics. Many centers offer well-structured programs throughout the seasons.

**GUESTMISTRESS – GUESTSISTER  – GUESTMASTER**  The person at a monastery or convent responsible for seeing to the needs of retreatants, and who is in charge of all aspects of hospitality, including making reservations and answering enquiries.

**HERMITAGE**   A place of solitude, silence, retreat, usually a simple abode where meals are taken alone in silence. A hermitage may be available for a day, a week or an extended period, depending on the facility's schedule. Some use this experience as a Prayer Sabbatical: a time to listen to the Spirit who is the real Director of the inner journey. Not recommended for those who have difficulty with being alone.

**LECTIO**   Receiving the revelation of God's love, especially in reading the Scriptures. In the monastic tradition it is part of the way of spirituality summed in the words: *lectio, meditatio, oratio, contemplatio.* Christian art works and audiotapes could be means to lectio. Lectio allows us to communicate with God. The most important aspect is one's desire, to open the mind and heart for Him to enter.

**MEDITATIO**   Meditation on the Word of God, on the images formed from sacred reading and study, touching the hearts of those truly seeking God, motivating and strengthening them to live a life in closer union with Our Lord.

**MONASTIC RETREAT HOUSE**   A contemporary response to St. Benedict's injunction to warmly receive guests as Christ Himself. Guests share in the daily round of prayer (q.v. Divine Office) and in daily Eucharist, and spend time in private prayer. Some monasteries provide for group retreats. A Spiritual Director may be available, and on a Directed Retreat there is daily contact with a Spiritual Counsellor.

**MONK**   A man in a community focussing on loving, honoring and serving God, and following a Rule (often an interpretation of the Rule of St. Benedict). Monks take vows of Poverty, Chastity, Obedience and sometimes Stability. Earnings and possessions become common property. Two key aspects of the common life are shared meals and the hours of prayer. Some monks are hermits (eremetical), but these are usually attached to a community too.

**NOVICE**   One entering a monastery or convent, choosing to offer the whole self to Christ. The novice gives up possessions and is clothed in the robe of the order. The novitiate lasts at least two years.

**ORATIO**   Prayerful response to God's speaking to us through Lectio and Meditatio. Our responses can be varied: repentance, or perhaps thanksgiving or praise.

**ORATORY**   A place of prayer where silence prevails.

**PILGRIM**   One who visits a holy place—a shrine, a place of deep spiritual significance. One who makes a holy journey to a sanctuary. Pilgrims often seek a stronger faith life or even a healing from a physical or moral problem. An atmosphere of reverence and silence is the norm.

**PILGRIMAGE**   A joyous community experience, finding the joy of Our Lord's house. An encounter with the sacred, a spiritual experience, a time of prayer and recollection.

**PREACHED RETREAT – CONFERENCE**   A spiritual program conducted by a retreat house or monastery. There is time for private prayer as well as community worship. Private consultation with a Retreat Director may be arranged by appointment.

**PRIVATE RETREAT**   The retreatant organizes his or her own time apart, usually has access to a library, and is welcome to worship with the community. If requested, a nun or monk or retreat house staff-member often is available to talk. Usually one must stay in the retreat house grounds or close by (nature walks etc.) Silence prevails for most of the retreat. For those seeking solitude. As with other retreats, the private, individually directed retreat can help in deepening awareness of God, and in searching for and finding answers. A time to rest in the Lord, get away from it all, relax, to get to know oneself and God.

**REFECTORY**   The dining room where the community and usually guests gather for meals–a time to nourish the body and soul. Many communities have readings or sacred music during meals.

**RELIGIOUS ORDER**   A distinct group of monks, nuns, priests or friars such as the Benedictines (Order of St. Benedict), the Dominicans (Order of Preachers), the Carmelites (Order of Discalced Carmelites) etc. who follow the Rule of a founder, and are organized in communities (monasteries, priories, convents), Congregations and Provinces. Regular General Chapters are held at which delegates from the communities from around the world meet. Most religious orders began in Europe during the Middle Ages. Some have dwindled, many continue to flourish, crossing national and cultural boundaries.

**RETREAT HOUSE**   A place where one makes a private or group retreat, of varying lengths of time. An environment of worship and calm where prayer, reading and contemplative quiet are encouraged. Meals are taken with the community unless otherwise specified.

**ROSARY**   'Beads' can be said formally, pondering the mysteries of faith with the *Hail Mary* as the primary prayer. Some simply hold the rosary while meditating or praying. A devotion prominent in the Catholic Church to honor Mary, the Mother of God. For many, a source of healing and peace. The devotion was revealed to St. Dominic when Our Blessed Mother said to him, "This land will always be sterile until rain falls on it." He understood that this rain was the devotion of the rosary, which he was to propagate.

**SABBATICAL**   Sabbath time, vacation time, a time for work or study without the usual worldly distractions. A time for contemplation, exercise and solitude. Solitude is extremely useful in deepening one's relationship with God, to evaluate one's commitment to Him, and to find wisdom and strength for gospel living.

**SAINT BENEDICT**   An Italian layman, Benedict of Nursia, who died around 545 A.D. at Monte Cassino, the abbey he founded. Holy Father of the monastic way of life in the west. Most religious orders of monks and nuns adhere to a version or a reformation of his Rule, written in the mode of *Lectio Divina*.

**SISTER**   Members of Religious Communities of women who do not make solemn vows, are called 'Sisters' rather than 'Nuns.'

**SPIRITUAL DIRECTION – GUIDANCE**   Many retreat houses provide this service, usually in keeping with a directed retreat. A member of the community meets with the retreatant once a day to set up and carry out a plan of spiritual activity: readings, prayer, assistance in interpreting the Holy Spirit's movements in one's life. This is a time to seek and find answers and to deepen one's prayer life. All through Christian history people have sought mentors from whom they could learn about discipleship and growth in the knowledge and love of God. The experience can become a journey together in searching for the truth of God's call and presence in each individual. By appointment, some retreat houses offer direction at times other than during a retreat, such as a 30-day Ignatian retreat in daily living.

**WAY OF THE CROSS**   According to tradition, The Blessed Virgin and early Christians would retrace the steps of Our Lord's Passion, sorrowfully meditating on those places or 'Stations' sanctified by the suffering Christ. In the Middle Ages, the faithful took long pilgrimages to the Holy Places to venerate that 'Way' which Jesus had travelled. From the 15th century, the Stations of the Cross were reproduced all over the world, allowing Christians to express the devotion often.

# HOUSES OF PRAYER
# & RETREAT CENTERS
# IN THE U.S.A.

HOLY SPIRIT RETREAT HOUSE
10980 Hillside Drive
Anchorage AK 99516
☎ 907 346 2343
Contact: Receptionist

Guests or retreatants of all religious traditions are welcome. Single and twin rooms. Individual winter guest rate: $40 per day; $60 for a shared room. Health-conscious kitchen. Meal service provided to groups of 20 or more.

GUEST RULES: Silence in sleeping and common areas during retreats. Smoking in designated areas only.

Rental facilities are available to non-profit organizations, private businesses, and individuals on a space-available basis. The Lounge can comfortably accommodate day group meetings of 15-20 people, casual seating, piano, kitchenette. Conference Room can accommodate up to 60 people, theatre-style seating, arranged to suit group needs.

DIRECTED SUMMER RETREATS: These offer opportunity for personal renewal. Focussing on the Spirit's movement and presence in each individual. In an atmosphere of silence and relaxation, conducive to prayer, retreatants follow their own daily rhythm which may include community prayer and Eucharist, and an individual direction session. Cost: $40 per day. Length of stay: one day to one week, depending on individual need.

The Retreat House is on 22 acres of forested land populated by moose, overlooking Anchorage and Mount McKinley. 24 hours of daylight during summer, Northern Lights in winter. A Stations of the Cross trail winds through the woods. The Resurrection Chapel provides a panoramic view of Anchorage, and a beautiful setting for prayer. Located 7 miles from Anchorage airport, 1.5 miles from Alaska State Park and ski area, 2 miles from Alaska Zoo.

Call or write for further information and to make reservations, including information on the Challenge Program—a 35-week retreat based on the Spiritual Exercises of St. Ignatius of Loyola. No deposit is necessary for retreats.

ST. JOHN ORTHODOX CATHEDRAL
P.O. Box 771108
18936 Monastery Drive
Eagle River AK 99577
☎ 907 696 2002
Contact: Pastor, or Assistant Pastor

At present there is one guest bedroom available for visitors. On 55 acres, which includes a church school, a cemetery, the 'Big House', and a half-mile walking trail to St. Sergius Chapel. More than 50 families of this Church live within walking distance of the Cathedral, creating a vital Church Community. The Cathedral was completed in 1984, most of the work being done by Church members.

The Cathedral has a 60 foot diameter geodesic dome. The wood of the ceiling is native Alaskan birch, and the altar furnishings are of Canadian cherry.

In April 1987, the Church Community which had been in Eagle River since 1975, was received into communion with the Orthodox Church under the Patriarch of Antioch. It shares the same historic faith and worship as all Orthodox Christians throughout the world.

Orthodox Christianity was first brought to Alaska in 1794 by Russian monks who came as missionaries. Today there are over 80 Russian Orthodox Churches in villages from the Aleutians to the Southeast Panhandle.

# ALASKA

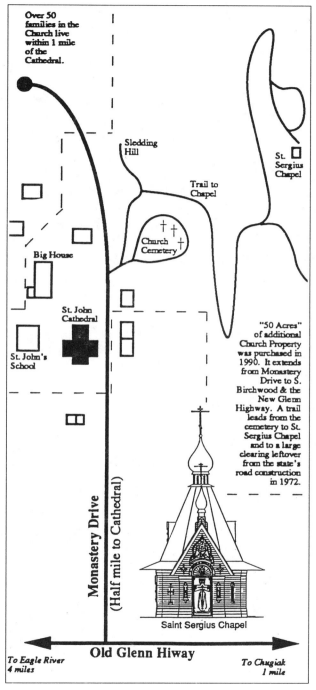

Over 50 families in the Church live within 1 mile of the Cathedral.

Sledding Hill

Trail to Chapel

St. Sergius Chapel

Church Cemetery

Big House

St. John Cathedral

St. John's School

"50 Acres" of additional Church Property was purchased in 1990. It extends from Monastery Drive to S. Birchwood & the New Glenn Highway. A trail leads from the cemetery to St. Sergius Chapel and to a large clearing leftover from the state's road construction in 1972.

Monastery Drive
(Half mile to Cathedral)

Saint Sergius Chapel

Old Glenn Hiway

To Eagle River
4 miles

To Chugiak
1 mile

3

SHRINE OF SAINT THERESE
5933 Lund Street
Juneau  AK 99801
☎ 907 780 6112
Contact: Director

PRIVATE RETREATS: 3 cabins. Two are rustic, with woodstoves and no indoor plumbing. The third has indoor facilities with gas/oil stoves.

GROUP RETREATS: Log lodge with accommodations for 23.

The Chapel is located on Shrine Island. St. Therese is the patroness of Alaska. This special place of pilgrimage is on Lynn Canal, 23 miles from Juneau, 13 miles from the airport and 10 miles from the ferry dock.

Call or write for further information and to make reservations

SERVANTS OF CHRIST PRIORY
28 W. Pasadena Avenue
Phoenix  AZ 85013
☎ 602 248 9321
Contact: Guestmaster

Quiet days and private retreats for those who want to share the ordered life of liturgy and worship, and to have quiet time in prayer and reflection. There is daily Eucharist and the office is said four times a day. Spiritual direction is available.

The Priory is staffed by Episcopalian Benedictines living in community. It is situated in easy reach of downtown Phoenix. A good library and modern chapel is available to retreatants. $45 per day.

REDEMPTORIST PICTURE ROCKS RETREAT

| 7101 W. Picture Rocks Rd. | *Mailing Address:* |
|---|---|
| Tucson AZ 85743 | P.O. Box 569 |
| ☎ 602-744-3400   Fax: 602-744-8021 | Cortaro AZ 85652 |

Contact: Director

Picture Rocks Retreat is a Desert Spiritual Life Center, a place of prayer and solitude in the beautiful Sonoran Desert, high in the foothills of the Tucson Mountains. The staff is a community of men and women associated with the Redemptorists of the Oakland Province. This community of prayer and service is dedicated to providing a nourishing place of peace where one can discover and embrace the sacred.

A retreat is a withdrawal to a safe place, offering the gifts of *Time* and *Space* for the Holy Spirit to lead us to a deeper and more intimate union with the true Spiritual Director—God, whom we call Teacher and Beloved. Through prayer and reflection the heart is opened to the spirit and one becomes a whole person ready to return to the secular world, refreshed and strengthened.

Located on 75 acres, 4 miles from Interstate 10, northwest of Tucson, and adjacent to the Saguaro National Monument West, the area features ample opportunity for the desert hiker and naturalist. There are miles of desert trails, shrines, and an outdoor Way of the Cross. This is also the site of ancient Hohokam Indian rock art (petroglyphs).

OVERNIGHT FACILITIES: comfortable private rooms with baths, prior registration is required, since these are limited. Group retreats: overnight accommodation for 85 people. Current rates for private retreats: $40 first day, $35 for each additional day. Includes linens, three meals a day, and time with a spiritual director if requested. Shuttle service is available from both Tucson and Phoenix airports for an additional fee. Call or write for current program and further information.

INDIVIDUAL DIRECTED RETREATS: Retreatants proceed at their own pace with the assistance of a director. Direction is given daily. Prior application and acceptance are necessary due to limited availability.

*Redemptorist Picture Rocks Retreat continued.*

PRIVATE RETREATS: Facilities provide an excellent atmosphere for prayer and solitude. Private Retreats can be made without the aid of a director. A private retreat facilitator is available to help in planning a retreat.

DAYS OF RECOLLECTION: Plan your own, or as a group, or attend one of the Center's scheduled events.

In addition to your own schedule of private prayer, retreatants are welcome to join the Picture Rocks community for Morning Praise, Eucharistic Liturgy, and Evening Prayer (Vespers).

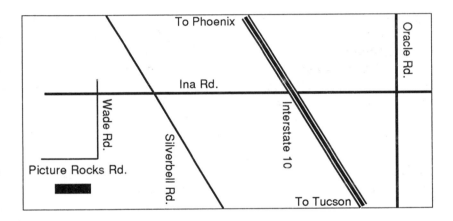

FRANCISCAN RENEWAL CENTER
Casa de Paz y Bien
5802 E. Lincoln Drive
P.O. Box 220
Scottsdale  AZ 85252
☎ 602 948 7460
Fax: 602 948 2325
Contact: Retreat Coordinator


The Franciscan Renewal Center, named Casa de Paz y Bien (House of Peace and All Good) was founded in 1951 by the Franciscan Friars. The 20 acre-site is set in scenic mountain-desert in Paradise Valley near metropolitan Phoenix. The Casa presents retreats, adult education classes and weekend workshops, and is also available to local, regional and national groups for educational, religious and humanitarian seminars.

The Center is a 20 minute drive from Sky Harbor International Airport. The surroundings include a private desert walkway, Meditation Chapel, a pool, spa, and spacious gardens. Because of the schedule of programs, the Casa is not suitable for a fully-secluded or silent retreat, but it does provide opportunities for quiet reflection in a friendly and accommodating atmosphere.

Piper Hall is a fully-equipped meeting center, with 4 conference rooms for up to 120 people. Audio-visual equipment is available can be reserved. There are several other conference rooms within the Center.

The Main Dining Room seats 150 people for buffet meals prepared in Casa's kitchen. There is a panoramic view of the rose gardens and Mummy Mountain.

There is sleeping accommodation for 110 people. All Rooms, which are in several different buildings, have a private bath and individually-controlled heating and air-conditioning. Most rooms are on ground-level and all walkways are stepless or ramped.

INDIVIDUAL RETREATS: The retreatant finds his or her own rhythm of prayer, reflection and relaxation, in an atmosphere of quiet and calm, and may participate in classes, workshops and conferences provided by the Center.

*Franciscan Renewal Center, continued*

INDIVIDUAL GUIDED RETREAT: Minimum 3-night stay. Regular meetings with a spiritual director for private discussion. Together you can plan definite hours of prayer, Bible-reading, times of reflection and periods of rest and relaxation.

PRAYER: Daily Mass at 7:00 AM. 5 Masses on Sunday. Morning Prayer, Monday to Friday. Vespers during Lent and Advent.

Casual, comfortable clothing, walking shoes, swimsuits are suggested. Linens are provided. Meals are included in the cost. Dine alone or join the staff in the dining-room.

Optional personal activities may include mountain-climbing, swimming and jogging. The Casa has a well-stocked bookstore and gift shop, and a limited audio-video library. In loving memory, guests have access to many books from Fr. Lambert Fremdling's private library.

Register at least 2 weeks in advance, giving alternate choice of dates. Space is not guaranteed without a deposit and confirmation from the Retreat Office. Phone or write for complete details.

*'Come apart unto a desert place and rest a while.'* Mark 6:31

DESERT HOUSE OF PRAYER
P.O. Box 574
Cortaro AZ 85652
☎ 602 744 3825
Contact: Director

Desert House of Prayer offers Private Retreats, Sabbaticals, Days of Recollection, Centering Prayer Retreats and the Hermitage Experience.

It is a place of prayer an contemplation. There is daily Eucharistic celebration and Liturgy of the Hours. All are welcome to join the community in its worship. Each retreatant is encouraged to engage in the classical steps of prayer: Lectio, Meditatio, Oratio and Contemplatio. There is a Night Vigil before the Blessed Sacrament from Saturday evening to Sunday morning. Spiritual Counselling is available on request.

There are two wings of living quarters. The Chapel of Our Lady of Solitude has large windows looking out onto the desert and surrounding mountains. There is a large community building with common room, kitchen, dining room, office and store rooms. There are also three self-contained hermitages.

As Teresa of Avila put it, the lifelong project of the Christian, and by inference, any well-adjusted person, is being neither solely contemplative nor solely active, but rather both at the same time—being both Martha and Mary.

Desert House of Prayer is a place of solitude set in 31 acres of primitive high desert land, covered with desert flowers, plants and trees, at the foot of Safford Peak in the Tucson Mountains.

A non-refundable deposit is required to confirm a reservation, which is applied to room and board. Full payment required on arrival.

Call or write for further information.

SAINT SCHOLASTICA CENTER
P.O. Box 3489
Fort Smith  AR 72913
☎ 501 783 1135
Contact: Sr. Cabrini Schmitz OSB, Center Director

The St. Scholastica Center is available for Private Retreats and Workshops.

Private Retreats: $30 per day per person, $50 per couple.

6-Day Guided Retreats: $175.

Weekend Retreats and Workshops: $75.

Call or write for further information.

Love turns work into rest.

**THE ABBEY RETREAT**
Coury House
Subiaco Abbey
Subiaco  AR 72865
☎ 501 934 4411
Contact: Rev. Aaron Pirrera OSB, Director

Subiaco Abbey is a Benedictine monastery, established in the 1800s. It was destroyed by a fire in 1927 and rebuilt. This is a special place of pilgrimage, in a pastoral setting.

The guesthouse is near the Pine Grove, where there is a Stations of the Cross shrine. There is a self-guided walking tour. Each room in the guesthouse has a private bath. There is a bookstore and gift shop, and a swimming pool for the summer months.

Write or call for more information and to make reservations.

O

Living Flame

of Love,

Holy Spirit,

the more

the soul desires You,

the more

it possesses

You!

St. John
of the Cross

HOLY TRANSFIGURATION MONASTERY
The Monks of Mount Tabor
17001 Tomki Road
P.O. Box 217
Redwood Valley  CA 95470
Contact Fr. Joseph

This is a Byzantine Catholic Monastery, open for Private Retreats only.  Write for further information.

SAINT ANDREW'S ABBEY
31001 North Valyermo Road
Valyermo CA 93563
☎ 805 944 2178
Contact: Guestmaster

Private Retreat, Group Retreats, Seasonal Retreats, Tours and Days of Recollection, are conducted by Benedictine monks who invite you to share their life, worship and silence.

Guesthouse facilities include 17 double rooms with twin beds and private bath. Linens provided. Rooms are air-conditioned in summer and heated in winter. There is a spacious lounge available for lectures, conferences, and informal meetings. Blackboard, VCR, coffee & tea provided by prior arrangement.

The Ceramic shop and the Art Shop with a large stock of spiritual books, tapes and gifts, are open daily. The Annual Fall Festival is one weekend that is unsuitable for a quiet retreat.

Monday–Friday suggested donation: $45 per night per person for a double, $50 for a private room—includes 3 meals daily. Weekends (Friday afternoon–Sunday afternoon) suggested donation: $100 per person, double, $120 for a private room. Homestyle meals are shared with the monks, breakfast is taken in silence. No pets allowed at the monastery.

Silence has always been one of the basic elements of monastic tradition and groups are invited to establish a curfew hour for night silence in rooms. The lounge is open all night, and the Chapel is open 24 hours for prayer, meditation and personal dialogue with the Lord. Guests are welcome to join the monks in chanting the Divine Office. Community Eucharist daily at noon. Groups can use the Chapel for services outside monastic hours.

Valyermo is in the northern foothills of the San Gabriel Mountains on the edge of the Mojave Desert at an altitude of 3600 feet, about 30 miles S.E. of Palmdale, CA. The change of seasons is very much a part of life at Valyermo. Be ready for warm days and cold nights. Informal dress is acceptable if restrained by a sense of propriety.

Reservations are required. Call between 9–11:45AM or 1:30–5PM, any day of the week. *See map overleaf.*

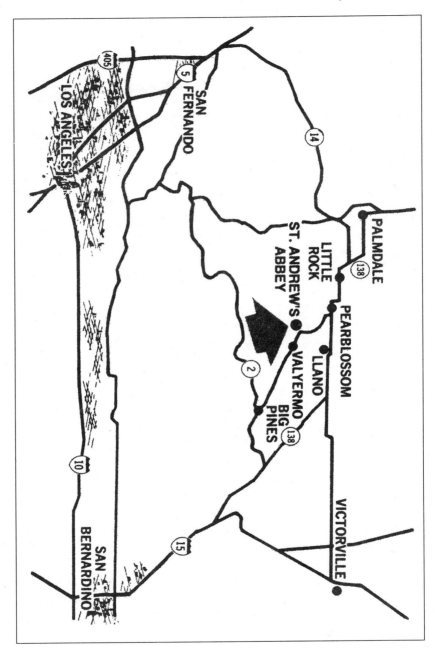

## COMMUNITY OF SAINT FRANCIS
3743 Army Street
San Francisco  CA 94110
Contact: Sister Jean, C.S.F.

One two-room apartment is available, with living area, kitchen and bedroom, for a single person or married couple on a short stay. The house is quiet but the street is busy.

A donation is welcomed. A letter of recommendation from a priest, sister, minister, or other person in ministry work is appreciated. Write in advance for reservations.

Prayer consists in loving much.

# IMMACULATE HEART COMMUNITY

Center For Spiritual Renewal
888 San Ysidro Lane
Santa Barbara  CA 93108
☎ 805 969 2474
Contact: The Director

The Center provides a place of rest, to reflect, to be renewed, and to realize God's gracious gifts of beauty, love and life. It is situated in a large stone house, 90 miles north of Los Angeles and 340 miles south of San Francisco.

*Private Retreats:* Six rooms are available for individuals or couples who wish to make a private retreat. People from a wide variety of religious backgrounds are welcome on a space-available basis, for stays of 2–5 days.

Guests are free to schedule their time to best suit their needs, with as much silence and solitude as they wish. Many spiritual books and tapes are available. Members of the Community are open to dialogue, if desired. All are welcome to join the evening communal prayer. The evening meal is served family-style at 6PM. Breakfast and lunch are pick-up at your leisure.

The Center is open from Wednesday morning to Sunday afternoon. Call or write for reservation form and further information, three months in advance. A $10 non-refundable deposit reserves a room. The Center operates on a donation basis. Average daily expenses: $45 for a single person, $55 for a married couple. Inability to make a donation should not keep one from seeking a needed time of reflection.

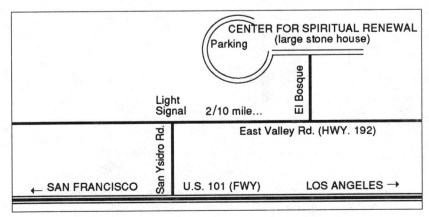

SHRINE OF SAINT JOSEPH
Oblates of St. Joseph–California Province
544 West Cliff Dr.
Santa Cruz  CA 95060
☎  408 427 1614 –Provincial
☎  408 423 7658 –Community
fax 408 457 1317

The Shrine was built in 1951 and dedicated in 1993. It has a magnificent statue of St. Joseph and the Child Jesus.

MASS: Monday–Saturday 11:00AM. Sunday 11:30 AM.

CONFESSION: Half an hour before Mass each day.

NOVENA TO ST. JOSEPH: Each Wednesday after Mass.

BOOKSTORE: Open before and after Mass.

The Shrine is open during the day, and all are welcome to visit. There is no overnight accommodation. If a group wishes to make a pilgrimage, the Congregation of priests and brothers can arrange a special talk or services.

Call or write for further information, including a history of this Congregation, founded in Italy by Bishop Joseph Marello who was beatified on September 26th, 1993, and is known as Blessed Joseph Marello.

# MOUNT CALVARY MONASTIC RETREAT HOUSE
P.O. Box 1296
Santa Barbara  CA 93102
☎ 805 962 9855

Mount Calvary is a Retreat House of the Order of the Holy Cross, a monastic community within the Anglican Communion Individual Retreatants are welcome from Monday afternoon through Friday afternoon, for overnight stays and up to four-day retreats. 30 spaces are available. Weekends are generally reserved by groups, several months in advance.

The Retreat House is a  Spanish Colonial Mansion set on a ridge overlooking Santa Barbara, with a 50-mile view of the coast. There is good hiking in the vicinity. Double rooms have private baths, single rooms have connecting baths. Cost, includes room and board: $50 first night, $45 thereafter.

Arrangements can be made for you to be met at the airport, or the bus and train stations, for which an additional donation is appreciated.

Call or write to reserve a space.

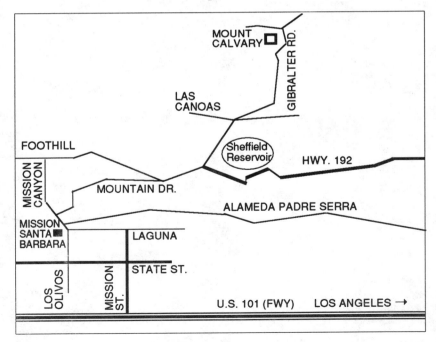

LA CASA DE MARIA
800 El Bosque Rd.
Santa Barbara CA 93108
☎ 805 969 5031
Contact: Program Coordinator

La Casa De Maria is an Ecumenical Retreat and Conference Center founded by the Immaculate Heart Community and governed by a multi-denominational board of trustees. It is a place of peace where persons of all faiths can search for truth, engage in dialogue, experience personal growth, realize their self-worth, embrace the sacred, and then, refreshed and renewed participate more responsibly in the creation of a just and peaceful world and a whole and healthful earth.

GROUP CONFERENCES: A schedule of programs is available on request.

WEDNESDAY RETREAT DAYS: From 9AM to 3PM. Times of quiet and times of sharing are part of each retreat day. There is no fee for the day, but a donation is appreciated. Lunch is available for $7.75 (reservation required), or bring your own lunch. Inform the Center if you plan a Retreat Day.

Partial scholarships and commuter rates are available for some programs—please enquire.

NEW CAMALDOLI HERMITAGE
Lucia
Big Sur  CA 93920
☎   408 667 2456 (2341)
fax: 408 667 0209
Contact: Guestmaster

The Hermitage is set in the Santa Lucia Mountains on 800 acres, at an elevation of 1300 feet, overlooking the Pacific Ocean and surrounded by woods. It is the home on the West Coast of the Camaldolese monks, founded in Italy about a thousand years ago by Saint Romuald of Ravenna, following the Rule of St. Benedict.

Nine rooms are available for men and women. There are several separate hermitages. Meals are vegetarian, and are eaten privately. An offering of $40–$50 per night is suggested, $300 for a week. Retreatants may join the monks for Mass and the Liturgy of the Hours. There is a well-stocked bookshop.

The Hermitage is located off Highway 1, 25 miles south of Big Sur, 55 miles south of Monterey, 85 miles north of San Luis Obispo. The nearest airport is in Monterey. There is no public transportation to the Hermitage, but between 4PM and 6PM on Fridays only, a driver can pick up at Monterey airport or bus station.

# CARMELITE HOUSE OF PRAYER
P.O. Box 347
Oakville  CA 94562
☎ 707 944 2454

PRIVATE RETREAT and DIRECTED RETREATS: 2-day minimum stay. WEEKEND RETREAT: $80 –a deposit of $10 is required, and two-weeks advance notice.

Also available: Small Group Retreats, Mornings of Recollection –every first Saturday, Poustinia Weekends (fasting and solitude). Special Programs can be arranged on request. Ecumenical and Inter-faith Prayer Groups are welcome.

The Carmelites trace their spiritual origins back into the Old Testament times of the Prophet Elijah on the mountain of Carmel. The Carmelites of Oakville provide space, community lifestyle, and an atmosphere which facilitates the wonderful, hidden and mysterious contact with God.

Oakville is 12 miles north of the city of Napa, and six miles south of St. Helena on Highway 29. Santa Rosa is to the West. Along the backroads of Northern California, in the heart of the Napa Valley, this House of Prayer is one of those out-of-the way places (Mark 6:31) where one can find rest and refreshment in the company of the Lord.

# MARIAN RETREAT CENTER
535 Sacramento Street
Auburn  CA 95603
☎ 916 887 2019 (2048)
Contact: Director

The Marian Retreat Center is sponsored by the Sisters of Mercy of Auburn, and is dedicated to the Spiritual Enrichment of all Persons of Faith. The Center offers loving hospitality to individuals and groups whose philosophy  and beliefs are in harmony with the purposes and values of the Center. We sponsor opportunities to enhance a spirituality grounded in Christian tradition and responsive to the needs of our times.

The Sisters of Mercy of Auburn, through the Marian Retreat Center, witness to the belief in God who acts directly and concretely in the lives of all people; we urge those who come, to love God and all creation in truth and justice.

The Center is situated on 33 beautiful acres in the Sierra Foothills East of Sacramento, and is used for conferences, retreats, workshops, days of prayer and/or spiritual direction. There are large and small conference rooms, a meditation room, library, auditorium, two chapels, dining room, 41 private bedrooms,  swimming pool, tennis court and basketball court.

ONGOING PROGRAMS:

*The Spiritual Journey: Christian Growth & Transformation.* Weekly, Tuesdays 9:30AM–11:30AM.

*Lectio Divina Prayer and Classics of Christian Mysticism.* Bi-weekly, 1st and 3rd Wednesdays, 7:15PM–8:30PM.

*Sitting Prayer Meditation.* Bi-weekly, 2nd and 4th Mondays, 7:30PM–9:00PM.

Call or write for further information.

INDIVIDUAL DIRECTED RETREATS:

Quiet retreats on a one-to-one basis by experienced retreat/ spiritual directors, from a few days to a month. Include a daily meeting with your Director to reflect on your retreat experience and what is happening in your prayer, and to receive guidance in ways to proceed, and help in prayer and discernment. Directors are prepared to accompany others through the Spiritual Exercises of St. Ignatius and in adapting them, or other prayer methods according to the needs of the individual. Each Directed Retreat is individually scheduled.

DAYS OF PRAYER and/or OVERNIGHT MINI-RETREATS with Spiritual Direction are available.

Ongoing, regularly scheduled individual Spiritual Direction with qualified Spiritual Directors is offered as a special service of the Center

A non-refundable deposit is required to secure your reservation: $25 for a weekend, $15 total for single days. All donations are considered offerings, and no-one is turned away for lack of funds. Feel free to enquire about scholarships.

Write or call for further details and for the current schedule of retreats/workshops.

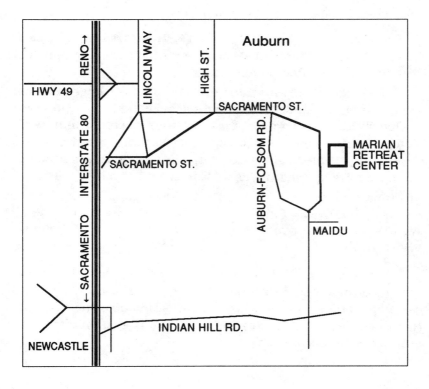

BENET PINES RETREAT CENTER
15780 Highway 83
Colorado Springs  CO 80921
☎ 719 495 2574
Contact: Sr. Olive Therese Geiger OSB

Benet Pines Retreat Center exists in order to provide a quiet environment to call people to gather, to receive Benedictine hospitality, to allow each individual to discover more fully God and themselves, and to experience the majestic gifts of nature in a wooded mountain setting.

The Benedictine faith Community extends to all faiths an invitation to gather in prayer through private, provided, or scheduled retreats, in order to become renewed and refreshed.

The Benedictine faith Community at Benet Pines promotes a prayerful, hospitable and quiet environment, where persons of many religious persuasions may gather to discover more fully their God, themselves, and each other.

The Center provides for Directed Retreats, Private Retreats, Group Retreats, Sabbaticals and Mini-Sabbaticals. Spiritual Direction is available on request.

Centering Prayer —a means to grow into a deeper personal relationship with God. One's attention is centered on the presence of God within. It is a prayer of interior silence. Opportunities for Centering Prayer practice and instruction include: Daily Community Centering, Weekly Support Group, Introduction to Centering Prayer, and Intensive Centering Prayer Retreats.

Monastic Days and Ways of Prayer —a community experience of Lectio Divina, Faith Sharing and simple lunch: each Wednesday 7:30AM–11:30AM. Donation accepted. Call for more information.

Accommodation is available in 3 hermitages; one small cottage with 4 bedrooms (for 6 people), a living room and kitchen; and one new cottage with 4 bedrooms (double occupancy), living room and kitchen. A large 40-person hall is available for day-use. Write for current rates.

Benet Pines is easily accessible from Denver or Colorado Springs by car, bus or plane. Arrangements can be made for pick-up at the airport or bus depot. The Center is located in a beautiful rustic setting in 30 acres of pine in the Black Forest.

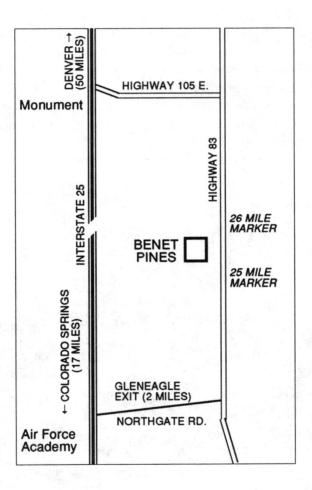

HOLY CROSS ABBEY
P.O. Box 1510
Cañon City  CO 81215
☎ 719 275 8631
Contact: Guestmaster

The Benedictine Order of Monks (Roman Catholic) at Holy Cross Abbey provide for INDIVIDUAL and GROUP RETREATS.

Over 100 guests can be accommodated in single and twin-bedded rooms with shared bathrooms. Meals are included.

The Abbey is set in 200 acres, some of which is used as farm-land. There is a monastery, guest houses, chapel, gift shop and library.

Located on U.S. Highway 50, 2 miles east of Cañon City and 38 miles west of Pueblo, near the San Isabel National Forest.

Call or write for further information and reservations.

Holy Cross Abbey    CANON CITY, COLORADO

**QUEEN OF PEACE ORATORY**
5360 Columbine Rd.
Denver CO 80221
☎ 303 477 9139
Contact: Sister M. Elenius, Director

The Queen of Peace Oratory provides for guided or directed retreats of two days or more.

The Oratory is located northeast of downtown Denver, on Route 287, near Regis College.

Write or call for more information and reservations.

*Where there is no love put Love and you will find love.*

Saint John of the Cross

ABBEY OF SAINT WALBURGA
6717 S. Boulder Rd.
Boulder CO 80303
☎ 303 494 5733 (Mon-Sat. 9–11AM & 2:30–4:30PM)

The Community is of cloistered Benedictine nuns, observing silence. Guests are asked to respect this atmosphere whilst at the Abbey. Retreatants are welcome to attend Daily Eucharist and to participate in the Divine Office which is chanted seven times each day in the Abbey Chapel.

Guests are encouraged to open themselves to God in silence, prayer, reading, and the beauty of nature in the 150 acres surrounding the Abbey.

GROUP RETREATS and PRIVATE RETREATS are available: Day and Weekend Retreats, Evenings of Reflection, and study series on Biblical, Liturgical and Theological topics. There is a variety of programs rooted in the Benedictine tradition of Scripture Study, Liturgy and The Arts.

Presentations on monastic life and tours of the Abbey Church and farm area are available on weekday mornings for school field-trips and other groups. A donation is appreciated.

The Guesthouse can accommodate 30–40 overnight guests in single and shared rooms. Three meals per day are served cafeteria-style in the guest dining room of the main Abbey building. Facilities include: meeting rooms, chapel, library, lounges, art and book shop. No smoking.

Suggested donations:
Individual Retreat (room & meals): $35 1st, $30 following nights.
1 night, no meals: $20 single or shared, $25 married couple.
1 day, without room or meals: $5

A bus runs hourly from Denver International Airport to the Table Mesa Park-and-Ride on S. Boulder Rd., about 2 miles west of the Abbey. Local bus #227 can be taken from there to the Abbey. There is also an airport shuttle to Boulder.

The nuns at Saint Walburga support themselves by hosting retreat groups and private guests. They also grow hay and other feed crops on 150 acres, and raise cattle and llamas for sale. An atmosphere of prayer, quietude and rural serenity prevails in the farm and at the Abbey. The Abbey has a fascinating history which is described in a brochure. A complete schedule of retreats and suggested donations is available on request.

*The Community's Coat of Arms: a red Benedictine Cross symbolizes the Abbey, standing at the foot of the Rocky Mountains. In the field of blue Colorado sky above, St. Walburga is represented by three silver drops, recalling the holy oil that flows from her relics, which are preserved at the Motherhouse in Eichstätt, Germany.*

NADA HERMITAGE
Spiritual Life Institute
Crestone CO 81131
☎ 719 256 4778
Fax: 719 256 4719

Nada Hermitage offers a unique environment for a wilderness retreat. It is located at an altitude of 8000 feet in the majestic Sangre de Cristo Mountains, overlooking the expansive desert of the San Luis Valley.

Our society has become overcrowded, over-protected and over-civilized. No one can live a fully human life without some experience of the wilderness. In the Judeo-Christian tradition, the desert, the mountains, the forest and other solitary places are used synonymously to refer to the basic wilderness experience.

Life here is a rhythm of work and play, solitude and togetherness, fast and feast, discipline and wildness, sacrifice and celebration, contemplation and action.

Retreatants participate in the monastic rhythms or choose solitude in their own hermitages. All are welcome.

Each well-balanced person has inner resources that often remain untapped. The Spirit within will ordinarily be your director, but a monk is also available at the beginning of your retreat, for minimal direction that does not detract from the basic wilderness experience.

Retreatants work with monks and other guests on Saturday mornings doing chores. Manual labor is available at other times, and is encouraged, especially when one is here for a long stay.

To make a reservation for a personal, minimally structured retreat, write and suggest dates—beginning on a Thursday and ending on the next Wednesday—and include some information about yourself. Your are welcome for as long as a month. Submit alternate dates in case your first choice is full. Your reservation is not confirmed until you receive a letter back from the staff. Arrive between 1–4 PM (before Vespers) and depart on a Wednesday by noon.

Bring rugged clothes year-round, warm clothing during the winter months, and your own tape recorder if possible. There is an excellent library of tapes and books. Bedding and simple food is provided. Be prepared to cook most of your own meals in solitude. Each hermitage has a kitchen and bathroom.

Nada Hermitage is accessible by car or air. If you go by air, fly into Denver and catch the connecting flight to Alamosa. Staff can pick up at Alamosa, but there may be a need to wait depending on arrival/departure times and other retreatants.

Crestone is located 1 hour north of Alamosa, or 1 hour south of Salida on CO 17. By car: 4 hours south of Denver, 5 hours north of Albuquerque, and 3.5 hours southwest of Colorado Springs.

Hermitages are $50 for the first day, and $40 for each additional day. Couples may share a hermitage for $60 the first day, and $50 for each additional day. If more can be afforded, it will be deeply appreciated, since Nada Hermitage is still under construction.

**FRANCISCAN CENTER**
Mount St. Francis
7665 Assisi Heights
Colorado Springs  CO 80919
☎ 719 598 5486
Contact: Director

Mount St. Francis is the Motherhouse of the Sisters of St. Francis and the location of St. Francis of Assisi Parish, The Franciscan Center, St. Francis Nursing Center, and the Franciscan Family Wellness Program.

The Franciscan Retreat and Conference Center provides a quiet, reflective atmosphere for prayer, private retreat, workshops, seminars, or just a relaxing time away. The Center has been completely renovated to enhance the Franciscan tradition of Hospitality. There are large and small conference rooms. Lodging includes single, double, triple, and handicapped bedrooms, all with private baths, for a total of 74 beds.

Nestled in the foothills of the Rockies –fresh mountain air and hiking trails, this is a place where one can be renewed spiritually and physically. Guests are welcome to visit the Chapel for prayer and to join the Sisters in Community Prayers and Mass.

Prices as of January 1994: $25 per night. $13 for 3 meals. Call or write for complete details about the facilities.

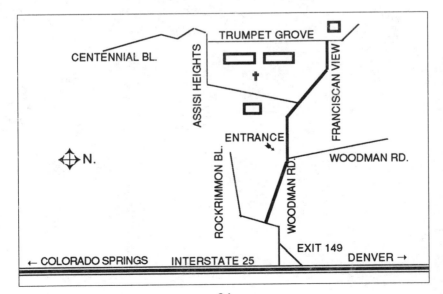

CARITAS HOUSE
House of Prayer
Elizabeth, Colorado

Contact:
Fr. Tom McCormick
6690 E. 72nd Ave.
Commerce City  CO 80022
☎ 303 289 6489

Caritas House is a place of quiet, situated in the middle of a ranch. Accommodation for up to six people consists of a modular home with 3 bedrooms, two bathrooms. A free-will offering.

Call or write for further information.

SHRINE OF OUR LADY OF LOURDES
AND RETREAT HOUSE
P.O. Box 667
Litchfield CT 06759
☎ 203 567 1041
Contact: Shrine Director
*Staffed by the Montfort Missionaries*

DAY PILGRIMAGE: 11:30AM Mass at the Grotto, 12:30 Lunch, 1:30 Way of the Cross, 3:00PM Rosary and Benediction.

EVENING OF RECOLLECTION: Mass at 5PM or 7:15PM, Supper: 6PM.

TOUR BUS GROUPS: Specify time of arrival, and whether you wish a guided tour.

Catered Meal Reservations: These are prepared by Shrine Volunteers. Reserve at least 1 month in advance, $25 non-refundable deposit. Group Leader to specify number of catered meals, at least 4 days in advance of pilgrimage date. Send for reservation form.

The principal Shrine at Lourdes in Litchfield is the Grotto of Our Lady, constructed of local fieldstone in a natural rock ledge, and modelled after the actual Grotto in Lourdes, France. The Shrine grounds are open year-round to the public. Devotion Services and Pilgrimage Programs are held from the first Sunday of May until mid-October.

A highlight of the Shrine is the winding and ascending WAY OF THE CROSS which culminates in the Crucifixion scene that dominates the entire Shrine area below.

Located on the 35-acre grounds, in natural settings, are Shrines of the Sacred Heart, Saint Michael, Saint Jude, Saint Joseph, and Saint Louis de Montfort.

Activities can take place daily at the Shrine, and are not affected by inclement weather. Mass can be offered in the PILGRIM HALL in place of the Grotto.

There is a Gift Shop, and ample parking for cars and buses. Adjacent to the parking lot is a picnic area with tables and fireplaces for the convenience of pilgrims and visitors. Handicapped people are welcome.

*Shrine of Our Lady of Lourdes, Continued*

*Come to me, all you who are weary and find life burdensome, and I will refresh you.* Matthew. 11:28

The pilgrimage we make in this life is towards the Promised Land which is Jesus Christ. To symbolize this journey, Christians throughout the centuries have made pilgrimages to the holy places of Christ's life to express in visible form their inner journey to the Promised Land of Heaven where Christ is our Life: *God loved us so much that He was generous with His mercy; when we were dead through our sins, He brought us to life with Christ...and raised us up with Him and gave us a place with Him in Heaven, in Christ Jesus.* Ephesians 2:4–6

Holy places or shrines, in Church tradition, have made us reflect on the role of Christ in our lives. Often, because they have been sites of miracles in Our Lady's name, or have been erected in her honor, they have pointed out to us the role of Mary in leading us to salvation in Jesus Christ.

The Montfort Missionaries' Shrine, Lourdes in Litchfield, has been constructed to foster devotion to Jesus through an understanding of Mary as the Perfect Christian, or First Pilgrim in the Heavenly Jerusalem. Mary is one with us in our faith; she is the woman of faith who stands with us on our pilgrimage to fulfillment in the Lord.

As followers of St. Louis de Montfort, a missionary priest who labored in France in the early 18th century, the Montfort Missionaries have attempted to implement, in our own times, their founder's vision of the role of Mary in the Church. By establishing the Shrine in Our Lady's honor, the Montfort Missionaries hope to lead Christians to full devotion to Jesus in union with the First Christian, the Blessed Virgin.

*To know Jesus Christ the Eternal and Incarnate Wisdom is to know enough: to know everything else and not to know Jesus is to know nothing.* —St. Louis de Montfort, from his first book: *Love of Eternal Wisdom.*

**AVE MARIA PLACE**
Diocese of Norwich
376 Putnam Rd., Route 12
P.O. Box 242
Wauregan CT 06387
☎ 203 774 0278
Contact: Fr. Pat Martin, Director

Ave Maria Place is a 'Come Aside and Rest Awhile' spot in rural northeastern Connecticut. It is 6 acres of peace, prayer, laughter, rest, sharing—located just 2 miles from Interstate 395, exit 89. A host family welcomes guests. The grounds are beautiful, thanks to the custodian and volunteers.

Ave Maria Chapel is always open for prayer. There is a guest house for your stay, a chapel/conference center for your meetings, there are outdoor chapels for your quiet and rest, a Way of the Cross and a Rosary Walk for prayer and contemplation.

Ave Maria Place is for those seeking space to find some peace, a quiet vacation, a day or an evening retreat for yourself or your group, or just to get away from it all for an hour, a day, or a few days.

Come find rest for body and spirit in a 'home away from home.'

For further details, call or write Fr. Pat Martin.

# UNITARIAN UNIVERSALIST IN THE PINES Inc.
Retreat Center
7029 Cedar Lane
Brooksville FL 34601
☎ 904 796 4457

*A Welcoming Place for Everyone.*

Near Withlacoochee State Forest, 1 hour from Tampa International Airport, 6 miles west of I-75 (Brooksville exit #61), UU in the Pines is situated in 13 acres of secluded, rustic woodland. There are rolling hills and orange groves, it is near the lake area of West Central Florida.

UU in the Pines welcomes Individual and Group Retreats, Conferences and Workshops.

3 Guest Houses sleep 60 people, shared bathrooms. The Lodge seats 100 people in the Great Hall, and includes break-out rooms, a library, dining hall, kitchen and unheated outdoor swimming pool. There is a small Peace Chapel on the Nature Trail. Buildings are heated and air-conditioned. Restaurants are nearby. Meals are prepared for groups and kitchen facilities are available to individuals.

## MONASTERY OF THE VISITATION
Maryfield
2055 Ridgedale Drive.
Snellville GA 30278
☎ 404 972 1060
Contact: The Guestsister

A Desert Experience Within Cloister is now available to young ladies and mature women. Pray, sing, read, think with cloistered, contemplative nuns. The Monastery provides a time of silence and solitude for individuals who wish to be alone with the Lord for a little while: from two to eight days.

*"I will allure her and bring her into the wilderness and speak tenderly to her."* [Hosea 2:14]

Facilities for two or three retreatants, open on weekends and weekdays. The rooms are simple, separate from the sisters, but in the enclosure. There is a small library and reading room. Meals are taken in the refectory with the Community. Spiritual reading or tape recordings played during meals. The monastery is situated on 26 acres including two wooded areas and a small pond. Ample space for walking, and facilities for relaxing out of doors.

Retreatants may participate in the prayers of the Community. There is Daily Mass. The Liturgy of the Hours is chanted five times a day. A sister is in charge of retreatants —she is appointed to speak with those who wish it, but will not intrude on one's strict solitude if that is desired.

*"Prayer is simply a loving talk between the soul and God."*
St. Francis de Sales

*"Prayer is a hidden manna, neither known nor valued save by those who come by it, and the more we taste it, the more our relish for it grows."*
St. Jane Frances de Chantal

GOD'S COUNTRY FARM Inc.
2222 Country Farm Lane
Blairsville GA 30512
☎ 706 745 1560
Contact: Bill and Arlene Gray.

God's Country Farm offers peace and tranquility in a country mountain setting. It is open May through October, and is recommended by: The Christian Family Center, RD 1, Box 259-F Holly Ridge, NC 28445.

Accommodation consists of 3 modern log cabins each sleeping 2-6 people, on a 50-acre Guest Farm, with fully-equipped kitchens, covered porches, rocking chairs, and gas BBQ grills.

There is a private fishing pond, animals, fruit trees, blackberry bushes. Down the road is Lake Nottely and a boat ramp and pontoon boat.

## ASCENSION PRIORY AND MINISTRY CENTER
541 East 100th South
Jerome ID 83338
☎ 208 324 2377
Contact: Rev. Joseph Wood OSB, Guestmaster

The Retreat Guesthouse can accommodate 16 people at present, plus 12 guests in the Priory building. Located in Southern Idaho. Call or write for further information and to make reservations.

# MARYMOUNT HERMITAGE
2159 Hermitage Lane
Mesa ID 83643
Contact Sister M. Beverly HSM

Founded in 1984 for a new contemplative community of Catholic women hermits, the Hermit Sisters of Mary, who live by the Rule of St. Benedict. The purpose of the hermitages is strictly spiritual, they are open to men and women who wish to share in the life of prayer, solitude and silence.

Marymount Hermitage is 125 miles northwest of Boise, one mile along a dirt road off Highway 95. It is set in 100 acres of rolling high desert range land, never cultivated, donated by the Ball family of Mesa, ID. This is scenic wilderness area at an elevation of 3200 feet, surrounded by mountains, on a mesa overlooking a valley, a place of solitude, with hiking, bird-watching and wildlife.

There is a chapel, library, community house, a garden and workshops, 3 hermitages for sisters and chaplain, and 2 hermitages for retreatants. Each is fully furnished and secluded, self-catering, using community staples, or bring your own food. No smoking. Parlor, laundry and supplies in the Common House. One hermitage in cloistered area is reserved for women, especially those discerning a call to this way of life. Manual work is available and recommended for longer retreats.

Share in the prayer life of the Community in Daily Mass, Lauds and Vespers. The Chapel is always open for Eucharistic adoration. The Chaplain is available for the Sacrament of Reconciliation. Arrangements can be made on arrival for informal spiritual sharing with one of the sisters. But retreats are essentially solitary, without formal direction.

A solitary retreat can be made from 2 to 30 days. Arrangements can be made for eremitical sabbaticals for qualified applicants. Reservations are necessary, to use a hermitage. Send for an application and return it with a non-refundable deposit. Allow 2 weeks for confirmation for a visit or retreat of 2-7 days. Allow about 1 month to confirm 8–30 days retreats, two letters of recommendation are required. Cost: $30 per day + tax. When requesting application, send a business-size SAE with two stamps, a newsletter of retreatants' reflections accompanies brochure.

See brochure for information about climate, clothing and transportation, transportation fees and special dietary needs, if applicable.

NATIONAL SHRINE OF SAINT JUDE
Our Lady of Guadalupe Church
3200 E. 91st Street
Chicago IL 60617
*Write to:*
Novena Office
205 W. Monroe Street
Chicago IL 60606
Contact: Fr. John Lemrise, Novena Director
         Fr. Mark Brummel, Co-Director.


Open daily. Founded by Claretian Fathers in 1929, this is the 'mother' shrine of devotion to St. Jude in North America.

Call Chicago Transit Authority for directions: 312 836 7000.

There is ample lighted parking at the Shrine, but a scarcity of lodging and dining places in the immediate area of the Church. Check with Monastery of the Holy Cross (p.46 in this Directory).

St. Jude is the Patron Saint of difficult and hopeless cases. With a donated statue of the Saint, the Shrine began humbly in the 1920s, in a parish of steelworkers and their families hit hard by layoffs during the Great Depression. The Novena to St. Jude helped to lift their spirits. Crowds packed the church. A special vigil light room is adjacent to the St. Jude altar −1000 votive lights representing prayers of thanks and petition, from the patrons of the Saint.

Lights have played an important part in the Church since the days of the early Christians, with lighted candles at Mass and other liturgical celebrations. This custom may have begun with the ever-burning lights at the tombs of the martyrs in the catacombs, signifying unity with the Christians who remained on Earth.

There are five novenas made each year at the Shrine, − February, May, June, August and October. They testify to the magnetic appeal St. Jude holds for the faithful.

The largest first-class relic of St. Jude in North America is housed in the Shrine, and is presented for veneration at each novena. On the side of the altar, a reliquary contains a piece of the Saint's tibia, brought from Rome years ago.

*National Shrine of St. Jude, Continued*

Father James Tort had a particular devotion to St. Jude Thaddeus. When he founded the Shrine, St. Jude was relatively unknown to the general Catholic population, although during the Middle Ages, St. Jude was widely venerated. Word of devotions to St. Jude gradually spread from this tiny corner of Chicago to other parts of the country.

Novena literature is available from the Shrine Office for those who want to make a novena at home. The novenas at the Shrine include Claretian priests as well as guest preachers from other religious orders —distinguished clergymen who have delivered inspiring sermons during the novenas. Information about St. Jude and the Shrine will be sent on request.

Fr. Brummel finds the many petitions and letters of thanks to St. Jude through the years, a continuing source of inspiration. He says, "It is not a charismatic-type devotion. It's more of a silent kind of inner conversion." In total, the stories that flow into the Shrine Office represent a tremendous and tangible testament to the worthiness of prayer.

## MONASTERY OF THE HOLY CROSS
Monks of the Holy Cross of Jerusalem
1049 West 31st. Street
Chicago IL 60608
☎ 312 927 7424
Contact: Prior

A contemplative monastic community whose charism is to give a silent and prayerful witness in the heart of the city. Choosing to live in the city has meant giving particular emphasis to hospitality. Guests are welcome to participate in the full life of the monastic community, to the extent that they are comfortable. This includes use of library facilities, the church, and meals in the monastic refectory, together with the community.

St. Joseph's Loft, a cozy area separate from the monks' living quarters, accommodates retreatants and guests. It is a place of silence and prayer. No smoking.

The lovely Gothic-style monastic church seats about 100. Old oak choir stalls add to the dignity of the celebration of the Divine Office. The altar, made from old pews from the church, is a work of art.

The Monastery is in the Bridgeport (Southside) neighborhood of Chicago, directly off Highway 94. Easy access to public transport to downtown. An elevated train line facilitates travel to O'Hare and Midway airports. Chinatown and Comisky Field are nearby.

Call or write for further information.

## NATIONAL SHRINE OF OUR LADY OF THE SNOWS

Missionary Oblates of Mary Immaculate
9500 West IL Route 15
Belleville IL 62223
☎ 618 397 6700
   314 241 3400
Contact: Fr. William P. Clark OMI

This is one of the world's largest Marian Shrines. It is located just 15 minutes from downtown St. Louis. Visitors walk, pray and reflect within the Shrine's 200 acres of natural woods and beautifully landscaped devotional areas. It is open every day of the year to people of all ages and faith traditions. Admission free.

Daily liturgies, retreats, marriage and family programs, multimedia presentations, ministries to persons with disabilities, special events, and a variety of other pilgrim activities and services are part of the Shrine's calendar. Send for a calendar of events and further information.

Usually in talking of devotion to the Mother of Jesus under a particular title, there is a link, either to one of Mary's qualities (Mother of Mercy, Sorrowful Mother), or to one of her apparitions (Our Lady of Lourdes). Devotion to Mary under the title of Our Lady of the Snows has some ties to the legend about a marvelous snowfall in Rome in 352 A.D., after Our Lady had indicated to a Roman couple in a dream, where she wanted a church built in her honor. However, Our Lady of the Snows is honored here, not so much because of the legend, but because of her special role in a Church which is by its very nature, missionary.

The Missionary Oblates of Mary Immaculate, the order of priests and brothers who operate the Shrine, following the inspiration of their founder, Blessed Eugene DeMazenod, have always called upon Mary as their principal patroness and the one who looks upon their missionary efforts with a mother's love.

When visiting the Shrine, seek not only peace of mind and closeness to God for yourself; seek also Our Lady's intercession for the spread of the Gospel throughout the world.

*Go Into the whole world and proclaim*
*the Good News to all Creation.* Mark 16:15

## MARYTOWN
Kolbe Shrine
1600 West Park Avenue
Libertyville IL 60048
☎ 708 367 7800

Marytown Kolbe Shrine, is open to those wishing to make a private retreat. It is situated 40 miles from Chicago and 50 miles from Milwaukee.

A small guest house accommodates 22 people in single and double rooms. There is a beautiful chapel, seating 200, where there is Perpetual Adoration of the Blessed Sacrament.

Suggested fees: $20 overnight, $35 with meals. $60 for a weekend. Visitors may find accommodation here if space is available.

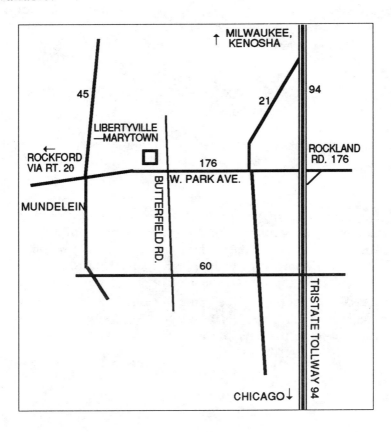

# HANDMAIDS OF THE MOST HOLY TRINITY
## MONASTERY – HERMITAGE
23089 Adams Road
South Bend  IN 46628
☎ 219 272 9425 (Call before 7:45PM EST)
Contact: Sr. Mary Emmanuel or Sr. Mary Magdalene

*Mary, Our Lady of the Sign, is a timeless model for all persons seeking a depth experience of God in prayerful solitude or in communion with others. Mary's experience is what our lives as contemplatives are all about. Our monastic presence is an oasis of lived spirituality, seedlike, yet ever in process of becoming that tree where all the birds of the air, all the nations may come to rest.*

For those desiring to make a Private Retreat, this is a Christian Contemplative Ashram seeking to integrate the Spirituality of East and West. Retreatants must stay on the grounds to enter into the silence and solitude, and are requested to share in creating an atmosphere of prayer and silence, which is vital in hearing the Word of God and keeping it, bearing fruit in Jesus' Name.

The sisters seek to share with guests their worship and prayer, in intense and joyful spiritual living, and invite those who seek to spend time with them to live as they live: simple quarters, simple meals.

Hermitages are available from the first week in May until the end of September. Facilities at the Ashram include a Contemplative Center, Chapel and Library. Usually guests bring their own food which they prepare themselves. Bring your own toiletries. A laundry and bed-sheets are provided. No alcohol, pets, or smoking in the hermitages, fields or bedrooms of the Center.

Other needs: soft slippers contribute to the atmosphere of silence; simple foods requiring minimum preparation and refrigeration; a Bible, raincoat, flashlight and alarm clock.

A donation is deeply appreciated and truly needed to maintain this holy place.

SAINT JUDE GUEST HOUSE
Saint Meinrad Archabbey
Saint Meinrad IN 47577
☎ 812 357 6585
Contact: Guestmaster / Tour Director

The monks of St. Meinrad treasure their long tradition of spiritual renewal and prayer, and recognize the value of taking time out to spend with God as essential for a healthy relationship with The Lord and our neighbors. They seek to share and promote this way to spiritual growth and they offer a variety of retreat opportunities throughout the year.

WEEKEND RETREATS are open to all Christian people, men and women, single, married, divorced and widowed. The suggested donation, including meals, is $90 for single occupancy and $150 for double.

MIDWEEK RETREATS are open to all Christian people, especially those who are retired, have free time, or are on vacation. Suggested donation, including meals: $80 single occupancy, and $120 double.

GROUP RETREATS by special arrangement. Groups of all kinds are welcome to use the Guest House and its facilities for their retreats and workshops.

GUIDED RETREATS provide a meeting with a Director once a day. In the Benedictine tradition, Scripture is used prayerfully to discern the workings of the Holy Spirit in one's life. Suggested donation: $50 per day, including room, meals, and Director's fee.

PRIVATE RETREATS are self-directed. These 'do-it-yourself' retreats give one the chance to experience some time alone with God. Suggested donation: $35 per day, including room and meals.

The Archabbey Guest House has 25 air-conditioned rooms with 2 twin beds, private bath, desk, phone, easy chair. Guest facilities also include a chapel, dining room, conference rooms and a lounge, Spacious grounds are available for running or walking.

*Saint Jude Guest House, Continued.*

All retreatants are invited to join the monastic community for the daily celebration of the Eucharist, and in praying the Divine Office in the Archabbey Church. Conferences and meals are held in the Guest House. Check-in time for retreats on Tuesdays and Fridays is from 2-5PM. Opening conference is at 7:45PM. Departure for both retreats is after lunch on Thursday or Sunday.

The Blessed Sacrament is reserved during scheduled weekend retreats only. The Guest House Chapel is open daily from 7AM until midnight.

Also available: Private Retreat videotapes; exercise equipment in Marty Gym; Library; Scholar Shop; Abbey Press Gift Shop; Monte Cassino Shrine; Self-guided tour; Audio-cassette tour; Guided tour.

No pets in rooms, lounges or dining area. Smoking is allowed in some areas.

For guaranteed room reservations, a non-refundable deposit of $20 is requested. Write for retreat schedules and hospitality information.

Saint Meinrad is located in southern Indiana, about halfway between Evansville, Indiana, and Louisville, Kentucky, and 150 miles south of Indianapolis.

## SAINT MARY OF THE ANGELS HERMITAGE
The Portiuncula
Mount Saint Francis Retreat Center
101 Saint Anthony Drive
Mount Saint Francis  IN 47146
☎ 812 923 8817
Contact: Fr. Jim Van Dorn, OFM Conv., Hermitage Director

Jesus often sought out quiet places to pray. St. Francis of Assisi sought out the solitude of the *Carceri,* a series of caves on Mount Alverna where he could commune with God. This tradition of withdrawing from the usual course of one's life for prayer and reflection, is being rediscovered by people from all walks of life.

St. Francis' favorite chapel, dedicated to St. Mary of the Angels, was nicknamed the *Portiuncula* (little portion). It was in the adjacent infirmary that St. Francis died on October 3rd, 1226.

Send for a Hermitage Questionnaire to fill out for approval to use the Hermitage. Usually two weeks' notice is needed to confirm the use of the Hermitage, and the maximum time spent there is one week. Retreatants meet with a Spiritual Director at the beginning of their Hermitage experience and set the time of daily meeting.

The usual stipend is $35 per day, which includes Spiritual Direction. Meals taken at the Retreat Center are extra – make arrangements prior to arrival. No food service on Sunday or Monday evenings. You may bring your own food,– microwave, utensils, etc. provided. The Hermitage has electricity, heat, small bathroom, linens provided. Shower available in lower level of Youth Center.

Casual dress and walking shoes are in order. A Bible or other form of spiritual reading is all else one may need. No radios, tape/C.D. players, alcohol, smoking, or pets. To preserve the solitude of the area, others are asked to avoid the vicinity.

Retreatants are welcome to join the Friars, Monday to Saturday for Morning and Evening Prayer in the Main Chapel, and daily Eucharist. Further information, with times of services will be sent on request.

# The Challenge of the Hermitage

The Hermitage is a type of desert experience. It is not always a place of rest; it can be a place of confrontation by God for our growth in his life and love.

The purpose of pursuing the Hermitage experience is to seek God and God alone. If that intention is primary, then I can enter the desert time unafraid, because I can be sure that God is there. If, however, I expect more from life than God alone, then I must not go to the hermitage or desert, for that more which I am seeking cannot be found there. The Hermitage is the testing ground for authenticity. There I can know for certain what it is that I am seeking—God alone, or God plus something else. Do I serve one master, or are there really two? In the desert or Hermitage there is only one Master, and the apparent sterility of my work there may be the only way to ensure that it is truly the Master whom I serve.

The friends of God have always been trained and tested in a desert of some sort. The Hermitage is such a place. And even if a person never goes to the Hermitage, he or she will sooner or later meet some type of desert where God will test for who the true Master is. Not even Christ could bypass the desert.

The Hermitage provides one type of desert where in our loneliness and solitude, we can clear away the illusions which prevent us from obtaining a clear view of all things that clutter up our heart. One cannot be in the hermitage for any serious length of time if one is not simple and poor in spirit, and if one expects from life something other than God alone. That is why the temptation to make ourselves useful to people in another way than just to show God's greatness and love, the temptation to establish the Kingdom of God by any means other than the ones Jesus used, can be ultimately overcome only in the desert, as Jesus did.

The reason the above meditation is offered for your reflection, is because we consider the Hermitage to be an unique spiritual time. It can be misunderstood and thus become a place for rest, study, a mini-vacation, etc. Although some of these things may happen just by being in the Hermitage, they are not the main reason, nor should one pursue lesser goals than The Lord.

If the Hermitage is not respected for what it means in the best Christian Catholic Tradition, it can be a great disappointment, and even unhealthy for those who just want to get away from things.

*The Franciscans at Mount St. Francis Retreat Center.*

GENEVA CENTER
5282 North Old U.S. 31
Rochester  IN 46975
☎ 219 223 6915
Contact: Manager

Geneva Center serves as a conference and retreat center for churches and non-profit groups, and is a summer camp for children and youth. Geneva Center exists to be used by God for God's own purposes. Our calling is to provide hospitality in a world that is all too often inhospitable, and to bear witness to the hope of God's Kingdom by modelling it in all our relationships.

Our speciality is providing hospitality for overnight conferences and retreats for groups as large as 130 and as small as 5 or 6. We also provide for one-day conferences or meetings. Although hospitality is offered in the name of Christ, there is no religious agenda for guests. Religious diversity is understood and respected, and secular contributions are celebrated in making God's world a better place.

Participants have the time to walk in the woods, to contemplate their personal and professional situations, and to enjoy getting to know each other. It is not so much a time to get away as it is a time to get back to things—back to the source and the meaning of life, back to having time to think and talk and plan. The staff is flexible and well-trained, and with advance planning is willing and able to help with the various components of your retreat program in a peaceful and relaxed atmosphere.

Geneva Center is a mission of the Presbytery of Wabash Valley. It is open to all those religious and secular organizations whose goals and purposes are not contrary to the goals and purposes of Christ's Church.

*Two Day Sabbatical for Professionals:* —an individual experience, to provide time and opportunity for the Church Professional to engage in uninterrupted work or study, with time for contemplation, exercise and solitude. The Sabbatical is open Mondays through Thursday, depending on availability. Phone reservations can be taken on very short notice and no paperwork or deposit is needed to reserve a space. Lunch and an evening snack are provided. Call for further information.

Both the cabins and the conference center are used by groups on retreat. The cabins offer a close-to-nature experience, while the conference center offers a little more luxury.

*Conference Center:* motel-style bedrooms for 64 people, with adjoining shower and restroom. Linens provided. Conference room for 75 people with 6 break-out rooms. Full meal service: homestyle, plentiful and tasty. Comfortable lobby and gathering spaces.

*Cabins:* 5 comfortable, winterized cedar cabins. Each sleeps up to 14 people. Fireplace in each cabin. Serene, wooded setting.

*Redwood Lodge:* A spacious activity center for 70 people, and a redwood deck for outdoor gathering. Restrooms in the Lodge.

Facilities also include an Olympic swimming pool open June 1st through Labor Day, 180 acres of conifer and deciduous woods, a campfire circle and a recreation field.

The Geneva Center is 40 miles from South Bend Airport. The staff can coordinate arrivals and departures there on seven national airlines. Call or write the Center for current rates and further information.

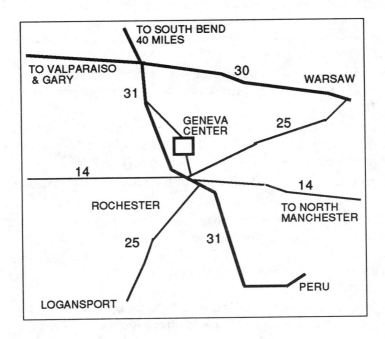

PROVIDENCE CENTER
St. Mary-of-the-Woods
IN 47876
☎ 812 535 4193
Contact: Bettye Lechner, Director

The Providence Center was founded in 1840 by the Venerable Mother Theodore Guerin and five companions. It is the home of 300 Sisters of Providence and of St. Mary-of-the-Woods College, the oldest Catholic Liberal Arts College for women in the nation. The architecture is Italian Renaissance, thousands of trees along pathways and avenues with abundant fauna provide a park-like setting.

There are several shrines and grottoes on the grounds, including: The National Shrine of Our Lady of Providence with Gaetano's portrait of Our Lady; the Our Lady of Lourdes Grotto; the 100 year-old church of the Immaculate Conception; the Blessed Sacrament Chapel, and the St. Anne Shell Chapel, decorated with iridescent shells from the Wabash River. For history buffs there is a Heritage Museum and Hall of Memories, and there are unique gifts and treasures made by the Sisters in the Gift Shop.

Individuals and families are welcome. Sunday is a good day to visit, a sumptuous buffet brunch is served from 10:30AM– 1:30PM.

Pilgrimages—days of spiritual awakening, renewal and prayer, can be arranged in advance. Group tours must be arranged in advance. Packages include tour and lunch.

Heritage Tour and buffet lunch, 21/2 hours, $7.00 per person.

Heritage Tour and private lunch, $10 per person.

Private retreats at Goodwin Guest House can be arranged by calling or writing Sister Ann Scott: 812 535 5274, or the Providence Center: 812 535 3131 Ext. 141. Write or call the Center for further information on the many facilities and places of pilgrimage.

The Center is a few miles from I–70, near the Indiana/Illinois border, 5 miles north of Terre Haute, Indiana.

# JOHN XXIII CENTER
407 West McDonald Street
Hartford City  IN 47348
☎ 317 348 4008
Contact: Director

This is a Retreat and Study Center sponsored by the Diocese of Lafayette-in-Indiana, a place where hospitality lives in a setting of peace and tranquility. People who share similar ideals of human and spiritual growth gather here in God's name. They leave strengthened, and renewed for service.

Facilities include a large, comfortable, modern house, a Chapel with open space, a large discussion room and three smaller visiting areas. There are kitchen and dining facilities for up to 40 adults and sleeping accommodation for 35 adults, or private areas for 14 couples, a spacious and colorful basement for larger group activities, a small library and reading room, and a bookstore.

The Center is flexible and adaptable to large and small groups for both Weekend and Midweek events. Cost: $25 overnight, including breakfast; $75 per weekend.

The John XXIII Center is for individuals and groups searching for spiritual and personal growth:

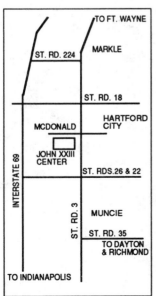

—Singles looking for new directions,
—Husbands and wives eager to grow in loving relationship with one another,
—Parents and teens desiring to strengthen their bonds,
—Catholics in search of a deeper faith,
—Ecumenical groups striving to grow in community and commitment to each other,
—Divorced and separated persons seeking new beginnings,
—College age students on a quest for meaning in their lives,
—Priests and ministers seeking spiritual refreshment, a place to share and grow,
—Women needing rest and relaxation and reflective time,
—Adult children of alcoholics and other persons healing the past,
—Persons committed to continual personal growth through reflection.

BEACON HOUSE MINISTRIES
915 North Third Street
Burlington IA 52601
☎ 319 752 2121
Contact: Guest Sister

A retreat center for private retreats and for small groups, located in a vintage house which accommodates 10 individuals or more if married couples are making a retreat. Three full-sized beds, the rest are twin beds. Retreatants prepare their own meals. Suggested donation: $15.

Call or write for reservations and directions and further information.

# NEW MELLERAY ABBEY
6500 Melleray Circle
Peosta IA 52068
☎ 319 588 2319
Contact: Guestmaster

New Melleray Guesthouse welcomes all retreatants regardless of sex, color, race or creed, offering an atmosphere of silence and peace which helps us hear the word of God speaking in our hearts. To help maintain an environment of silence, guests are asked to observe those times and places where talking or loud noises would be disturbing: no speaking in the rooms after 10PM, no musical instruments, TV, radios or cassettes without earphones. Guests are able to eat in silence at designated tables.

The area west of the Guesthouse (the front) is available for walking and exercise. Guests are not allowed in the monastic enclosure, including the farmyards. Tours of the monastery are no longer available.

Accommodations include 14 rooms with single beds, 4 rooms with twin beds, all have private baths, linen and towels provided. Small library and video room. No elevator. Children under 18 must be accompanied by an adult. Smoking is allowed upstairs.

Cafeteria-style meals are provided three times a day. There is a small room for tea, coffee and cookies. Breakfast at about 6:50AM after Mass, Dinner at noon, Supper at 6PM. Inform the Guestmaster if you will be absent from any meal, and also which will be your final meal. The dining room is closed after meals. Private retreatants during the week rise at 6:30 AM when chimes are sounded, and follow the above schedule for Mass and meals.

Retreats are private and are taken at any time from Monday noon, until Friday morning. On request, a priest is available to talk with retreatants. Weekend retreats are reserved for conferences which are booked a year in advance, but a last-minute call may secure an opening due to cancellation.

A free will offering is suggested.

In accord with the present discipline of the Catholic Church, reception of communion is limited to Catholics.

OUR LADY OF THE MISSISSIPPI ABBEY
8400 Abbey Hill
Dubuque IA 52003
Contact: Guest Secretary

Some retreat houses on the property for those who wish to make a private retreat. Retreatants do their own cooking, food is provided. Book well in advance. A free will offering is suggested. Please write for detailed information.

SOPHIA CENTER
801 South 8th Street
Atchison KS 66002
☎ 913 367 6110 (Ex. 204)
Contact: Sr. Johnette Putnam OSB, Director

Sophia Center is an extension of the ministry of hospitality of the Benedictine Sisters of Mount St. Scholastica, Atchison, Kansas. In addition to offering opportunities for days of quiet and solitude for the individual, formal retreats and workshops on spiritual themes are offered on a regular basis, and are described in a brochure published bi-annually. Retreatants are invited to join the Sisters for the daily monastic Hours of Prayer, as well as the Eucharistic celebration.

Room and Board: $25 per day; room only: $15. A Spiritual Director is available for an additional $10. A deposit of $15 is requested for all programs unless otherwise indicated on the Sophia Center brochure.

Atchison, Kansas, is approximately one-hour's drive north of Kansas City, Missouri.

SAINT BENEDICT'S ABBEY
Atchison KS 66002
Contact: Guestmaster

The Guest House can accommodate up to 16 people for individual retreats. $15 per night, $27 per night with meals.

Write for further information and reservations.

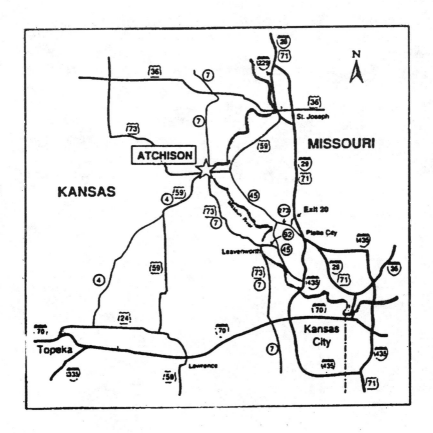

# ABBEY OF THE GETHSEMANI
3642 Monks Road
Trappist KY 40051
Contact: The Guestmaster

The Abbey of the Gethsemani has been receiving guests since 1848. Silence is the norm, talking is allowed only in designated areas. Guests are encouraged to assist at the Eucharist and the Hours of Prayer. A monk is available for consultation and the Sacrament of Reconciliation. For those who are interested, the Chaplain conducts conferences on various topics, and a presentation on monastic life. There is a library, and many acres of woods and fields. Meals are provided.

Midweek Retreats are between Monday morning to Friday morning, Weekend Retreats are from Friday morning to Sunday evening or Monday morning. Longer stays are exceptional. The minimum stay is two nights. The first and third full weeks of each month are reserved for women retreatants, and the rest of the month for men. Try to arrive before 7PM, E.T. Give notice if your plans change and you wish to cancel.

A free will offering is suggested to help operate facilities.

# MARYHILL RENEWAL CENTER
Catholic Diocese of Alexandria
600 Maryhill Road
Pineville LA 71360
☎ 318 640 1378 (M–F 9AM–4PM)
Contact: The Director

MISSION STATEMENT: Maryhill Renewal Center is *A Place, A People, A Presence.* Maryhill thereby promotes a Gospel response to the living out of God's love in service, leading to the renewal of persons who will serve the Lord within the Christian community. Through its natural surroundings, its programming, its personnel, Maryhill provides to all people, especially the Diocese of Alexandria, spiritual and educational opportunities for growth in holiness/wholeness. The staff of Maryhill Renewal Center extends to all who come hospitality, warmth and acceptance in the name of the Lord.

Maryhill is situated on a scenic and peaceful 190 acre woodland tract north of Pineville. Owned and operated by the Diocese of Alexandria, it is available to churches of all denominations, civic clubs and non-profit organizations for retreats, meetings, seminars and overnight programs. Business groups are also encouraged to consider this serene atmosphere as an excellent site for on-going education and an opportunity to get away from the hectic pace of life.

Modern motel-like housing includes 46 air-conditioned bedrooms with private baths. 3 suites are available for private retreats or a family 'get-away,' on a daily, weekly or weekend basis. Meeting rooms range from a parlor for 10-25 people, to a conference hall seating 150. Audio-visual equipment is available. Pine trees, the lake, a Way of the Cross, Marian patio, two chapels and prayer paths offer many ways to delight in creation. Catholic bookstore in the Administration building.

The Youth Ministry Center accommodates 110 people. A renovated pavilion, meeting room, dining room/kitchen allows groups the freedom to design an experience which best meets their needs. A pool, volleyball and basketball court, fire pit, and baseball field, along with prayer room and reflection points, give youth a variety of resources for re-creation.

The purpose of a retreat is to foster an ongoing process of prayerful listening and responding to the Spirit of God in the contemporary world; to help individuals and groups experience a deep commitment to the living Christ through development of the whole person.

Call or write for further information.

64

SAINT JOSEPH BY-THE-SEA
235 Pleasant Avenue
Peaks Island ME 04108
☎ 207 766 2284
Contact: Team Members
Conducted by the Sisters of Notre Dame

GUIDED RETREATS    Group spiritual guidance in a daily conference. Daily Liturgy and individual sharing with Director if desired.

DIRECTED RETREATS  Meet daily with Director for Spiritual Direction.

PRIVATE RETREATS  Personal retreat without Director. Retreat and music cassettes available. Daily Liturgy offered.

Contact the Retreat Coordinator for an application and detailed information. All retreats are conducted in an atmosphere of silence out of reverence for each other. Meals are taken in silence accompanied by music. Space for Vacation/Personal Renewal/Rest and Relaxation on request, subject to availability.

At St. Joseph's there are conference rooms, a large chapel, home-cooked meals, a sundeck, ocean view, a leisurely island life.

Peaks Island originally was divided into many parcels of land which were owned by several families. Oak Cottage, now known as St. Joseph-By-The-Sea, was built in 1864. The 28-room home is on high land, sloping to the bay and beach, a five-minute walk. The ocean side with breathtaking scenery and good fishing is ten-minutes walk away. From the eastern side of the island, there is an excellent view of the Atlantic Ocean. On both east and west sides, rocks, coves, spruce and pine woods afford ideal spots for rest and vacation.

Peaks is the best located and most populous of the more than 360 islands of Casco Bay. It is 3 miles from Portland, and has an area of 720 acres. It can be reached by the ferries of Casco Bay Lines.

DAYSPRING RETREAT CENTER
11301 Neelsville Church Road
Germantown MD 20876
☎ 301 428 9348
Contact: Director

All retreats at Dayspring Retreat Center are Silent Retreats for individuals and groups. The Center, with its Lodge of the Carpenter, is a gift from Him for Whom the Retreat Center, the Lodge, and the Church are all named. It is a rare and beautiful place where one finds seclusion, silence and rest for the reflection and prayer that deepens one's relationship with the One in Whom we live and move and have our being.

Believing that the world provides too little time and space for dialogue with God, and that prayer is central to the Christian life, the staff offers retreats as time set aside for contemplation. Here you will find a broad range of opportunities to deepen the spiritual journey. The leaders, men and women of mature personal faith, are experienced and skillful in guiding others through silence and meditation.

The Lodge and Inn, set amid the woods, fields and still waters of Dayspring, provide a quiet, comfortable place for meditation and prayer—a place prepared for you to commune with God in solitude.

WEEKEND RETREATS (Full retreats: 16 people), the fee is $90 per person, including $50 deposit, written application, no phone reservations. Arrival time: after 4PM, Friday, supper at 7PM., after which the retreat leader sets the theme and guides the retreatants in the Great Silence. Silence continues all day Saturday, a time of rest, contemplation, study, wandering or journal writing; one or two meditations by the leader offer guidance.

Corporate worship and sharing on Sunday leaving the Silence. The noon meal is taken together, departure at 2PM. Transportation between Dayspring and Metro is available at $5 per person, and can be arranged by calling in advance.

Weekend retreatants are expected to remain for the entire retreat. Bring toilet articles, warm casual clothes, walking shoes, flashlight and writing materials. No pets, alcohol, radios, or unnecessary valuables. No smoking in the Lodge or Inn. Simplicity is the aim.

*Dayspring Retreat Center, Continued*

We offer a simplified menu of natural, fresh foods, nutritionally balanced, plentiful and delicious. Bring your own food if you have special dietary requirements. The retreatant's choice to fast, a time-tested discipline for heightening spiritual awareness, is respected.

Other groups may use the Retreat Center for their own silent retreats. Write for further information.

INDIVIDUAL RETREATS are especially encouraged. For this personal time, bring your own food and be your own guide. Cost: $25 per night.

THE BELOVED RETREATS are offered monthly. They begin Sunday at 7PM and end Tuesday at 2 PM. Henri Nouwen's *Life of the Beloved* is the focus, and is required reading before the retreat.

EMBER DAY RETREATS–Reviving the ancient Christian tradition of quarterly Ember Days, these one-day retreats offer time, space and structure for weary servants, caregivers, and helping professionals. For many centuries, Ember Days, clustered at the four corners of the year, were occasions of prayer, fasting and renewal. These are offered as an antidote to the threat of Burnout. Through words, wisdom, and gathered silence, you will savor the gifts of each season, and seek to discern and draw on sources of replenishment to balance the energy drains in our lives.

MINI RETREAT–Begins at 10AM and concludes at 2PM. No charge, donations welcome, no reservation needed. Bring your own lunch and go to the Lodge of the Carpenter where a leader will open the retreat with a group devotion and meditation, and end with a brief sharing.

Send for the current program of retreats, registration forms and complete information about the various offerings at Dayspring.

MOUNT SAINT MARY'S ABBEY
300 Arnold Street
Wrentham MA 02093
☎ 508 528 1282 (Abbey)
   508 528 1620 (McMahon House–Frank Pariseau)
Contact: Retreat Coordinator

PRIVATE RETREATS –For single women, religious, clergy or married couples. Hospitality is offered to those who wish to share the monastic atmosphere of Mount Saint Mary's Abbey. Retreatants are free to use their time for prayer, reading, and visits to the Chapel where they can assist from the guests' section, adjacent to and separate from the Sisters' Choir.

Accommodations at the Abbey include a fully-equipped kitchen. Food basics are provided for you to prepare your meals as and when you wish. Bring any special dietary food you may require. There are supermarkets in the area. Arrive at the Abbey before 7PM.

McMahon Retreat House is a large house set in spacious grounds, a quarter of a mile up the road from the Abbey. Accommodations include 9 bedrooms some double, on 3 floors. On the first floor is a large dining room, a fully equipped kitchen and a spacious meeting room. A prayerful Meditation Room is on the third floor. A normal amount of food is provided for guests to prepare their meals. Extra food may be brought. Arrive at McMahon's by 9PM. Frank Pariseau is the resident custodian.

Call or write for complete information and reservations.

✠

Monastic communities exist not only to pray for the world, but perhaps more exactly, to stand before God *as* the world, His beloved but wounded creation, worshipping, seeking, being sought by Him, and finding its place in His heart.

The roots of this community reach back through their founding house, Glencairn Abbey in County Waterford, Ireland, through a line of Cistercian houses into the soil of France and a 12th century reform of the Benedictine observance. The Rule of Saint Benedict itself emerges from early 6th century Italy, reaching beyond to the deserts of Egypt, and further into the heart of the Gospel. The lifestyle of the Sisters is simple: liturgy, quiet prayer, manual labor, study, and the joys and challenges of community life.

*Mount St. Mary's, Continued*

Christian monasticism arose in a Near Eastern culture which held the guest sacred. Monks enriched this attitude with Christian insight, and received their visitors as the sacramental presence of Christ. Monasteries in former times have been sought as hostels on pilgrim routes.

Today, contemporary pilgrims of the heart find along their road a monastic guest house in which to refresh and clarify their journey in Christ. Days of monastic retreat can bring healing to the spirit, immersed in the silence of the Divine Mystery.

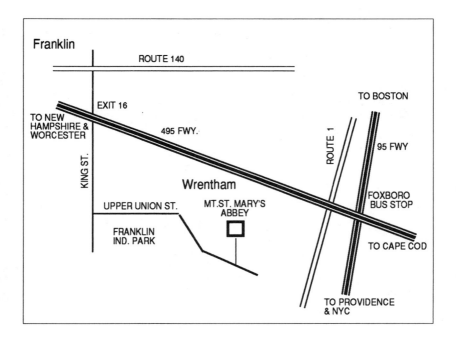

MARY HOUSE
P.O.Box 20
Spencer MA 01562
☎ 508 885 5450
Contact: Ms. Joyce Thomasmeyer

Mary House is owned and operated by lay people. It offers private retreats in silence for individuals and/or small groups, men and women of college age and older.

A lovely colonial house with spacious lawns and woods provides a unique and homelike atmosphere. There are minimal guidelines—come and go as you will. Supply your own food and prepare meals in the fully equipped kitchen.

The house is located on Route 31, 1/4 of a mile from the entrance to Saint Joseph's Trappist Abbey. It is 1 1/4 miles uphill to the monastery church.

An offering of $20–$60 per person per night is requested. Write or call at least two weeks in advance for reservations.

SAINT BENEDICT ABBEY
252 Still River Road
P.O. Box 67
Still River (Harvard) MA 01467
☎ 508 456 3221
Contact: Father Xavier Connelly OSB

Set in 75 acres of woodlands and farmland, overlooking the scenic Nashoba Valley, one hour west of Boston, the monastery is a 300 year–old Colonial home, decorated and furnished in that period. The Guest House is 250 years old. The whole area is steeped in Early American history.

Visitors may stay for one day to a week. A donation of $25 per day, including meals, is requested. 60 guests can be accommodated in single and twin-bedded rooms.

GENESIS SPIRITUAL LIFE CENTER
53 Mill Street
Westfield MA 01085
☎ 413 562 3627 (Sun.–Sat. 9AM–5PM)
Contact: Registrar

Genesis Spiritual Life Center offers hospitality to persons of all faiths, cultures and lifestyles. Genesis was founded in 1976 by the Sisters of Providence of Holyoke, MA. The Sisters, who own and administer the Center, are a community of women with more than a hundred years of service in the healing ministries.

The staff believes that when persons of different lifestyles and spiritualities connect, God's creative and healing energies are released. They have a special concern for those in the health and helping professions, for artists and craftspersons, and for those who feel alienated from church or society.

Programs are designed and hosted that foster holistic integration of body, mind and spirit. Each person is a seed of God–meant to grow into the likeness of God–and Genesis strives to be a place where that seed can be nourished and nurtured toward maturity.

Genesis' logo–the tree–reflects the belief that creation is ongoing and that each person always has the possibility of new beginnings in life and in prayer.

Set on 19 wooded acres, the Center combines sensitivity to atmosphere, devotion to the land, and carefully designed programs so all who come may experience God's providential care.

THEMATIC AND FOCUSING DIRECTED RETREATS: From a Genesis staff member. $40 per day, including room and board.

PRIVATE RETREATS: $30 per day, including room and board. Spiritual guidance is available.

SABBATICALS: Guests are welcomed for stays from one month to a year. Guests are encouraged to tailor their sabbaticals according to personal and specific needs. For those looking for a combination of silence and solitude coupled with opportunities to select programs from among the varied offerings at Genesis. Guests also take advantage of many cultural and educational opportunities in the beautiful Pioneer Valley and Berkshire Hills Sections of Western Massachusetts. Send for a brochure on the Sabbatical Program.

HOSTED PROGRAMS: Facilities are available to educational, medical, business, civic, religious and professional groups.

## *Genesis Spiritual Life Center, Continued*

REST AND READING DAYS: Every Tuesday, 9AM–5PM. $15, includes lunch and use of private room; $30 from Monday 7PM through Tuesday 5PM, includes breakfast and lunch. Conversation at meals only. Call or write for further information.

SUPPORT AND OTHER GROUPS: Space is provided without charge to those who gather to provide each other mutual help and understanding.

When possible, arrangements can be made for pick-up at Springfield bus and train terminals, or the Hartford/Springfield airport. $20 each way. Arrangements must be made in advance, giving the exact time of arrival. The Registrar can also help arrange ride-sharing. Call or write for registration form, current program calendar and further information.

The Center has a lovely 1889 Carriage House, flower and vegetable gardens and prayer paths for walking. There are double bedrooms for up to 55 overnight or weekend guests. Guests and retreatants staying for longer periods are assured a private room. Facilities include: two dining rooms, an air-conditioned chapel, library, fireplace room, meditation room and several conference and meeting rooms in the Carriage House.

The facilities are simple yet tasteful and the meals are home-cooked and nutritious. The spacious grounds enable guests to enjoy God–present and active in each of New England's four seasons.

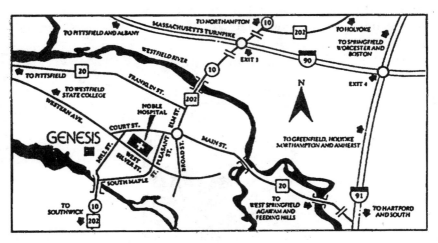

NATIONAL SHRINE OF OUR LADY OF LA SALETTE
251 Topsfield Road
Ipswich MA 01938
☎ 508 356 3151
FAX 508 356 3579
Contact: Ms. Tensi Boylan
Staffed by the Missionaries of Our Lady of La Salette and laity.

Open daily to visitors seeking a place of quiet and solitude. Sunday Liturgy 9:15AM.

Shrine Gift Store open Tuesday–Sunday, 10AM–5PM, (4PM in winter).

Pilgrimage bus tours are available for groups wishing to reserve a certain date to visit the Shrine. A program can be tailored to meet the needs of the group, including Devotions and Tours of the Shrine Chapel and grounds, formal gardens, and /or the Mansion on Turner Hill. A video presentation of the Apparition of Mary at La Salette, France, is available. Meals can also be arranged.

Newman Hall Retreat Center is located on the Shrine property. Retreats are scheduled throughout the year. The Center can be also rented by groups. Arrangements can be made by calling the listed contact person.

The Shrine is surrounded by acres of spacious grounds, duck ponds and gardens, lending itself beautifully to quiet walks and moments for reflection.

Call or write for further information.

GLASTONBURY ABBEY
16 Hull Street
Hingham MA 02043
☎ 617 749 2155 (M–F 8AM–2PM)
Contact: The Retreat Office

This community of Benedictine monks was founded in 1954. The Abbey is located in the historic town of Hingham on Boston's South Shore, less than 2 miles from the Atlantic Ocean, in a peaceful and beautiful environment on 60 wooded acres.

The retreat facilities at Glastonbury provide a contemporary response to St. Benedict's Rule of warmly receiving guests who come here to pray, to witness to a shared life of dedication to Christ, and to experience the joy, peace and love promised to believers gathered in His name. Guests share in the monastic atmosphere of prayer, silence and community, and are welcome to join the monks in their common prayer and daily Eucharist.

Individual and Group retreats are welcome throughout the year. Some special retreat programs are offered by the monks at special times during the year. Guests are guaranteed at least one individual meeting with a monk upon request.

There are two comfortable guest houses, informal and non-institutional in character. Stonecrest, the larger house, can accommodate up to 21 people; and Whiting House, a maximum of 8. There are private rooms for individual retreatants and a few rooms for couples. Both houses have fully equipped kitchens. The Abbey provides all meals for retreatants. However, in a spirit of community, guests are asked to help set tables and clean up after meals.

Suggested offering: for individuals, $40 per night for 2 or more nights, $45 for one night. A non-refundable and non-transferable deposit of one night's offering is requested to confirm reservation. For groups, the offering is $40 per night with a deposit of $200 to reserve the larger retreat house (minimum 15 people), and a deposit of $100 to reserve the smaller house (minimum 5 people).

Call or write for further information about retreats and retreat programs.

# SAINT JOSEPH'S ABBEY RETREAT HOUSE

Saint Joseph's Abbey
Spencer MA 01562
☎ 508 885 3010
Contact: The Guestmaster.

The monks are members of the Cistercian Order of Strict Observance (Trappists), a cloistered contemplative community following the 1500 year-old Rule of St. Benedict. Members of the Roman Catholic Church, the monks devote their lives to the cultivation of the presence of God in both solitude and community, since Christ is found in the silence of the heart and in commitment to communal life. They daily chant the praises of God in the Divine Office and the Eucharist, and devote themselves to private prayer, work and study.

While preserving the ancient traditions of monastic life with a lively and reverent enthusiasm, the monastery, settled in the pastoral landscape of New England, has always appreciated its place in the world of our time.

Guests may stay in this environment of worship and calm for a few days in the small retreat house adjoining the monastery, which has 11 private rooms each with a private bath. These ongoing retreats for men are offered mid-week: Monday afternoon to Friday morning; and on weekends: Friday afternoon to Sunday afternoon. Retreatants are not in direct contact with monks, but the house closely conforms to the atmosphere of the monastery. Prayer, reading and contemplative quiet are encouraged.

Retreatants attend daily Eucharist and Liturgy of the Hours. A light breakfast, lunch and supper are provided, as are conferences.

There is no set fee. Each may leave an offering according to his means, but it may be helpful to know that the average received ranges around $60–$150 per weekend, and from $150–$300 for midweek retreats.

The Abbey Retreat House is usually filled 6 months in advance and reservations are accepted only 6 months ahead. On the first day of any month, reservations are open for the whole of any month, six months ahead. Reservations are accepted only for two people at a time, and reserving by phone is preferred. The Guestmaster is available daily from 9–11AM and 1:30–7:30PM.

*St. Joseph's Abbey, Continued.*

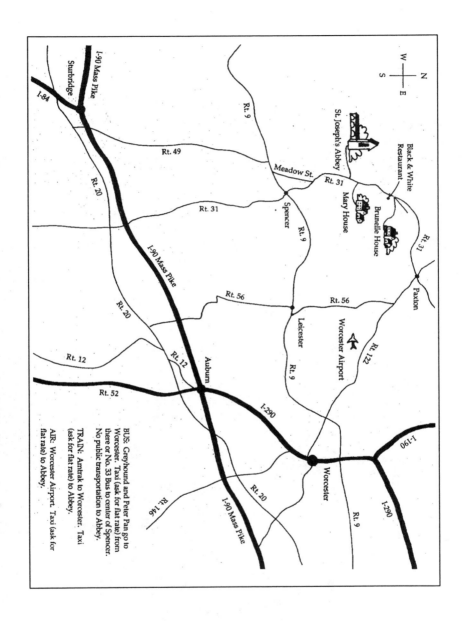

BUS: Greyhound and Peter Pan go to Worcester. Taxi (ask for flat rate) from there or No. 33 Bus to center of Spencer. No public transportation to Abbey.

TRAIN: Amtrak to Worcester. Taxi (ask for flat rate) to Abbey.

AIR: Worcester Airport. Taxi (ask for flat rate) to Abbey.

SAINT MARGARET'S CONVENT
17 Highland Park Street
Boston  MA 02119
☎   617 445 8961
FAX 617 445 7120
Contact: Guest Sister

St. Margaret's is a modern convent with a carriage house in the scenic and historic area of Fort Hill, close to downtown Boston and Longwood Medical area. It is the Motherhouse for the Society of St. Margaret, an Episcopal religious community for women. The Order welcomes families of medical patients, out of town guests, travelers and retreatants.

Guests may stay overnight, and meals are provided. Stays are usually limited to one or two weeks or shorter. Guests are encouraged to be in the convent by 9PM, but exceptions can be made.

Public transportation is a short walk away. There is parking on the convent grounds. The convent is at the top of a hill.

Suggested donation: $35 per night.

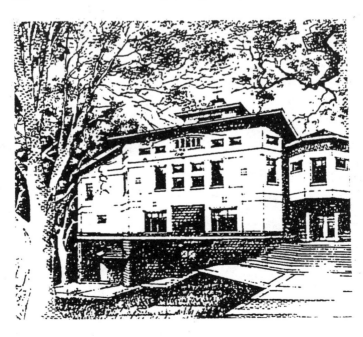

## SAINT MARINA'S GUEST HOUSE
71 Washington Street, Box C
Duxbury MA 02331 *[Summer address: June 15th—September 1st]*
☎ 617 934 5696

*Call or write:*

Saint Margaret's Convent
17 Highland Park Street
Boston MA 02119
☎ 617 445 8961
FAX 617 445 7120
Contact: The Guest Sister

St. Marina's Guest House is situated on the grounds of St. Margaret's Convent in South Duxbury, Massachusetts, 38 miles south of Boston of the South Shore.

Ten comfortable and quiet rooms, some double, are available. Six overlook Duxbury Bay. The house is open June 15th—September 1st, for a quiet retreat or vacation near the ocean on Cape Cod. Breakfast and lunch kitchen privileges, Dinner provided. $35 per night. No smoking. Parking on grounds. Daily Chapel service.

There is a private beach for swimming, and bicycles are provided for recreation. There is much to do and see in this historical area. Cape Cod is a delightful place to explore.

Write or phone in advance for reservations.

# THE SOCIETY OF SAINT JOHN THE EVANGELIST
Emery House
Emery Lane
West Newbury  MA 01985
☎   508 462 7940
FAX 508 462 0285
Contact: Guestmaster

Emery House is the home of members of the Society of Saint John the Evangelist, the oldest religious community for men in the Anglican Communion. It is located one hour north of Boston on 120 acres of fields and woods, bound by both the Merrimack and Artichoke Rivers and adjacent to a 400 acre state park.

Accommodations for 10 guests, 7 in private self-contained hermitages, and 3 in the main house, which dates from 1745

As the brothers form a community of prayer, they pray the Office and celebrate the Holy Eucharist daily. They ask that guests participate in their liturgical life at least once a day. They maintain an atmosphere of quiet in the house throughout the day. Most meals are vegetarian and are eaten in common.

The Community Sabbath Day is from mid-afternoon on Sunday until late afternoon on Monday, and the ministry of hospitality is not exercised at that time. Emery House is also normally closed for the first 3 weeks of June, all of September, and from Christmas until Epiphany.

Spiritual direction is available. A donation is asked of $45 per day, $55 if receiving spiritual direction from one of the brothers. A non-refundable, non-transferable deposit is required to reserve space. Write the Guestmaster for the Guesthouse program schedule or to make reservations.

## MONASTERY OF SAINT MARY AND SAINT JOHN
The Society of Saint John the Evangelist
980 Memorial Drive
Cambridge MA 02138
☎ 617 547 7330 or 876 3037
Contact: The Guestmaster

The Monastery of Saint Mary and Saint John is the main house of the North American Congregation of the Society of St. John the Evangelist.

Private retreats are offered Tuesday through Saturday. $45 per day, $55 if receiving spiritual direction from one of the brothers. There are 16 single bedrooms with shared showers. Vegetarian meals are included, taken with the community. Closed the first 3 weeks of June, all of September, and from Christmas to Epiphany.

The Brothers pray the Office and celebrate Holy Eucharist daily, and ask that guests participate in their liturgical life at least once a day. An atmosphere of quiet prevails.

The monastery guest house is a short walk from Harvard University and the Episcopal Divinity School —on the Charles River.

A non-refundable, non-transferable deposit is required to reserve space.

Call or write for a Guesthouse program or to make reservations.

Let nothing trouble thee
Let nothing frighten thee
All things pass away ✳✳
God never changes  ✤
Patience obtains all things
Nothing is wanting to him
        who possesses God
God alone suffices  ✤

        St. Teresa's Bookmark

✖

COLUMBIERE CENTER
9075 Big Lake Road, P.O. Box 139
Clarkston MI 48347
☎ 810 620 2534 or 810 625 5611
FAX 810 625 3526
Contact: Conference Coordinator

Columbiere Center is a retreat/conference center serving religious, educational and other groups for daytime and/or overnight non-profit programs.

Directed and private retreats for individuals are on a limited basis only. Spiritual Directors are available. Rate for individual retreatants: $30 overnight, with 3 meals. An additional stipend for spiritual direction would be agreed upon between the retreatant and director.

| GROUP CONFERENCE RATES: | SINGLE | | DOUBLE Per Person | |
|---|---|---|---|---|
| | Bath | No Bath | Bath | No Bath |
| Overnight/Weekday (1 night, 3 meals) | $53 | 48 | 49 | 44 |
| Overnight/Weekend (1 night, 3 meals) | 57 | 52 | 53 | 48 |
| Weekend (2 nights, 5 meals) | 92 | 82 | 85 | 75 |

*Rooms with private bath are air-conditioned. Limited availability.*

The above rates include the use of conference rooms, tea & coffee service provided morning, afternoon and evening. For those wishing to spend the day only (commuters) the rate is $10 per person per day, plus meals: breakfast $3, lunch $4.50, dinner $6.50.

The Center features buffet-style dining with reserved seating for up to 160 people in the main dining room, which overlooks the spacious grounds.

The Center's large chapel, where public Mass is celebrated each Sunday, is also available to conference groups for ecumenical services.

Columbiere Center is located on 400 wooded acres just outside the historic village of Clarkston, MI. Rolling hills, meadows and woods provide a peaceful setting away from the usual city distractions. The grounds feature nature trails, a baseball field, basketball court, and an indoor gymnasium. There is an outdoor swimming pool and picnic area with grills for summer and trails for cross-country skiing, and a pond for ice-skating in winter.

Contact the Conference Coordinator for further information.

AUGUSTINE CENTER
The Sacramentine Monastery
P.O. Box 84
Conway  MI 49722
☎ 616 347 3657
Contact: Administrator/Director

This is a diocesan center for education, on-going formation and spirituality. It is a Center for growth–to know the Lord better, to know His teachings more fully, to utilize that knowledge as a practical foundation of our lives and to place our personal gifts at the service of God and His people.

The Augustine Center encourages and hosts programs that focus on human growth and development. Retreats are Preached, Private and Directed.

Facilities include 40 bedrooms, each with a private bath, with shower, single or double occupancy. There are 11 additional bedrooms with semi-private baths, wash-basin in each room, single occupancy, linens provided. There are also 2 apartments each with 2 bedrooms and kitchen. Linens provided. 3 well-balanced meals a day are provided in a pleasant dining room.

The Prayer Room/sitting area is ideal for private retreatants and is conducive to reflective reading and meditation, with a beautiful view of the sunset. There is a Chapel for personal reflection and prayer, Eucharistic Liturgy, Sacrament of Reconciliation–open 24 hours.

The Conference Room for discussion groups or lectures seats up to 85 people. 9 lounges of varying sizes are attractive for breakout groups and various other activities.

The Augustine Center is located on U.S. Highway 31 North, overlooking Crooked Lake, with 22 acres of woods adjacent to the main grounds, 15 miles from the Cross in the Woods Shrine.

Call or write for further information and for current suggested donation for a retreat. A brochure and registration form will be sent on request.

HOUSE OF THE HOLY SHROUD
1629 Beach Road
Prescott MI 48756
Contact: Guest Brother

The House of the Holy Shroud is a Christian Guesthouse for private retreats. Men and women are welcome.

1 small guestroom with 1/2-bath on second floor; 5 small bedrooms and common bath on the first floor. If guest wishes to stay longer than 2 or 3 days, meals would be their responsibility. Free will offering for a short stay, for an extended stay there will be an arranged agreement.

The Guest house is located on 6 acres in a rural area, half wooded, no hunting allowed. It is on the less visited side of the Michigan Water Wonderland, so the atmosphere tends to be peaceful and conducive to prayer and reflection.

Write ahead for further information and to make your reservations.

## DORMITION OF THE MOTHER OF GOD MONASTERY
3389 Rives Eaton Road
Rives Junction  MI 49277
☎ 517 569 2873
Contact: Guestsister

The Monastery is an Orthodox Christian monastic community, the only Orthodox Monastery in Michigan. Founded by three Sisters who came from Romania to serve God, now the community has grown to ten. The monastery is a holy place in which to nurture the Spirit of God in us.

48 acres of woodland, with an array of wildlife, provide a perfect place for restoration and refreshment of mind, body and soul. The natural environment, quiet and tranquil, is a place of retreat from the stress of the secular world.

The daily cycle of services held in the chapel provides for the primary aspect of monastic life–to pray without ceasing. All visitors and guests are invited to attend the services or to send a list of names for intercessions to the monastery.

PRIVATE and GROUP RETREATS may be planned for one or several days. Limited overnight accommodations are available.

VISITORS FROM ALL FAITHS ARE WELCOME!

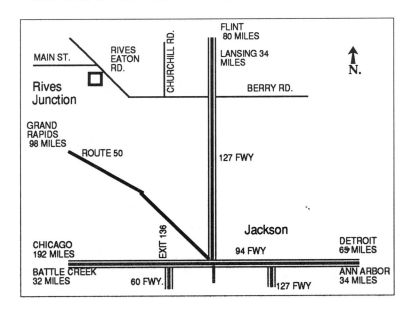

The Patronal Feast Day and annual pilgrimage of the monastery is the Feast of the Dormition of the Virgin Mary, celebrated in the Orthodox Church on August 15th. The Virgin Mary as the mother of the Incarnate God and as Intercessor before Him, takes an earthly presence in the icon of the Dormition.

Because of her closeness to God, having given birth to Jesus Christ, on her death her body did not remain in the tomb, but was resurrected and taken to heaven.

SAINT AUGUSTINE'S HOUSE
3316 East Drahner Road
Box 125
Oxford  MI 48371
☎ 810 628 5155 (Office)  810 628 2604 (Guest House).
Contact: Guestmaster

The Fellowship of St. Augustine was formed in 1956 by Fr. Arthur Carl Kreinheder, a recently ordained Lutheran clergyman who had just returned from several years of study in Sweden. There and in England and France, he had been exposed to a liturgical and monastic revival among Protestants as well as Roman Catholics. The Fellowship was formed to pray for, and to promote study, interest and understanding of religious life and to foster the establishment of a Lutheran monastic community. In the early days the Fellowship was an association for Lutherans and was largely clerical. However, its membership soon broadened as interest spread and as Fr. Arthur embraced the ecumenical movement. Today the Fellowship is open to all active Christians, men and women, clergy and laity. Members pray for and help to support the Congregation of the Servants of Christ, the Lutheran monastic (Benedictine) foundation at St. Augustine's House.

*Guest Information:* All are welcome to attend and participate in all liturgical services, and should normally be present for at least the Holy Eucharist, Sext, Vespers and Compline. Holy Communion may be received by all who are baptized, who desire to receive the true Body and Blood of Jesus Christ, and who are able to receive communion in their own church.

It is asked that all be respectful of the desire of some for silence and solitude. Certain periods of the day are set aside for silence. It is especially necessary to keep the upper level of the house as free from noise as possible after Compline in the evening and during the rest period in the afternoon.

*Meals and facilities:* Dinner and supper follow Sext and Vespers respectively. On ordinary weekdays, meals are taken in silence listening to a taped lecture or book at dinner and to music at supper. Meals are taken family-style. Breakfast is eaten in silence on a self-serve basis. Ordinary Wednesdays and Fridays are observed as fast days, and dinner is not served. Bread and simple foods are available after Sext for those who wish to serve themselves.

*St. Augustine's House, Continued*

Towels and linens provided. Smoking only out of doors. There is a library on the lower level for guests. Radio and tape players may be used at any time with earphones. TV in lower level may be ordinarily used only after supper and before Compline and Sunday afternoon.

St. Augustine's House is partially supported through the free-will donations of retreatants. There is no fixed fee for retreats. If you wish to make a retreat, phone or write for reservations.

*You have made us for yourself, O God, and our hearts*
*are restless until they rest in you.* –St. Augustine.

✠

*The Monastic Day* is punctuated by regular times of prayer. The roots of this tradition can be traced to the synagogue liturgy as well as to apostolic custom. Benedictine monastic prayer is inspired by two verses from Psalm 119 verses 62 & 164: *At midnight I will rise to give you thanks* and *Seven times a day do I praise you.* The times of prayer in a typical day at St. Augustine's House are described below. Members of the Fellowship may wish to relate their times of daily prayer to one or more of these traditional hours.

*Vigils* is the night prayer of the Church and is usually prayed in the early morning before the coming of light. After a brief interval, *Lauds,* or Morning Prayer is sung at 6 o'clock. This service celebrates not only the coming of earthly day, but more especially the *Dawn from on high,* the revelation of Jesus Christ, (Luke 1:68ff).

In the *Holy Eucharist* we give praise and thanks for our salvation accomplished through the death and resurrection of Jesus Christ. This is also the time that we intercede for the Church and the world. On Sundays, the Liturgy is celebrated at 10AM, and on weekdays usually at 8:30AM.

The course of the day is marked by three shorter times of prayer: *Terce,* before the Holy Eucharist, *Sext,* at noon, and *None,* in the mid-afternoon.

At Evening Prayer or *Vespers,* at 6PM, we turn to Jesus Christ, the unfailing light, and join with Mary in proclaiming God's greatness and mercy (Luke 1:46ff). The monastic day closes later in the evening with *Compline,* which prepares us for restful sleep and, on a spiritual level, for a peaceful and blessed death.

FULL CIRCLE HOUSE OF PRAYER
Sisters of Mary Reparatrix
2532 South Boulevard
Port Huron  MI 48060
☎ 810 364 3326
Contact: Directress

The Full Circle House of Prayer offers Spiritual Direction, Private and Directed Retreats, Retreats in Daily Life in the spirit of St. Ignatius Loyola, as well as ecological spirituality conferences, both on and off site.

---

*Guiding Beliefs*

There is an inseparable link between the integrity of creation, justice and peace.

Creation tends towards diversity.

All aspects of creation are worthy of respect.

All members of the Earth Community are interdependent.

Interdependence leads toward communion whose ultimate expression is love.

Contemplating these truths moves us to appropriate action.

---

Simple, beautiful accommodations include 3 private rooms, a chapel, library, fireplace, vegetarian meals, linens. There are two cats, Raggles and Ferdi, a raised-bed organic garden, herb beds, young trees, visiting birds, side walks and area churches extending an Earth Community welcome.

We are located an hour's drive north of Detroit, at the south end of Port Huron, in a long-established integrated neighborhood. The House overlooks a long, narrow park, a favorite fishing spot on the St. Clair River.

Send for the current rate schedule and to make reservations. There is a non-refundable deposit of 20% of the total cost, paid at the time of reservation.　　　　　　　•

## SPIRITUALITY CENTER
Sisters of Saint Benedict
104 Chapel Lane
Saint Joseph  MN 56374
☎ 612 363 7114  or  7112
Contact: Director

The mission of the Spirituality Center is to extend to others the spiritual, cultural, artistic and educational opportunities which the women of the monastic community create, develop and sustain. The Center provides programs, facilities, and human resources for individuals and groups of all faiths and cultures in an environment of Benedictine community, worship and hospitality.

Individuals or groups are welcome for a day or more retreat. Private rooms, sacred spaces and spacious grounds provide an atmosphere for recollection, reading and prayer. Retreatants are welcome to join the sisters in celebration of the Eucharist and Liturgy of the Hours.

Retreatants may bring their own food, follow the schedule of the community, or eat in the college cafeteria.

Spiritual Direction is available for those who desire assistance in understanding and responding to the movement of the Spirit in their lives. Directed Retreats or ongoing Spiritual Direction are available.

A Retreat is an age-old practice of withdrawing to a quiet place alone or with another, to take a look at life and sort things out. There is a need in the human heart to look back at life with reverence and gratitude and to look ahead with hope and generosity. A Retreat Center is a place, a setting, a symbol for our union with God and communion and compassion for others.

Write for further information and to make reservations. Suggested donation.

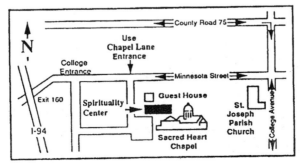

ARC RETREAT COMMUNITY
Route 2, Box 354
Stanchfield  MN 55080
☎ 612 689 3540  during office hours
Contact: Director

### MISSION STATEMENT:

The ARC Retreat Community is a Christian residential community and retreat center ministering to guests seeking rest and spiritual renewal in order to carry out their vocations in the world. Assisting the community in its ministry are Board members and other volunteers. ARC seeks to fulfill its mission by covenanting to:

Root its life in the Christian tradition through daily worship and regular eucharistic celebrations,

Seek the guidance of the Holy Spirit through listening and discernment in prayer and contemplation,

Encourage the gifts and resources of all in an inclusive and participatory sharing of work and community life,

Provide a safe, quiet space and gentle hospitality inviting guests to pursue their own spiritual journeys,

Pray and work for local and global justice, peace and ecumenism,

Offer a learning environment that fosters engagement with major life issues,

Emphasize a spirituality rooted in, and interconnected with all creation and embodied in a simplified and compassionate life,

Be open to and pioneer creative expressions of community, ministry, and life-style,

Live joyfully, simply, mercifully,

Be a sign of hope!

✠

A resident community of 6-8 people serves as the staff, providing hospitality, managing the house, arranging worship, leading retreats, preparing meals and performing the other services of the ARC's ministry.

The ARC kitchen is well-known for its wholesome, homemade food–simple, tasty meals respecting the global view that invites us to live more with less.

## *ARC Retreat Community, Continued*

The Retreat is an intentional time set apart for silence, attentive listening, and for opening oneself to the movement of God's Spirit in our lives. Retreat is not an escape from reality, but an opportunity to view reality differently. Time apart helps one to gain new perspectives, re-establish priorities, and to move beyond superficiality. Personal renewal comes through a deepened self engaged in a widened world. The journey inward (personal renewal) and the journey outward (social justice) are vital and inseparable aspects of the spiritual life.

Retreats are offered by the ARC Community or planned together with a scheduled group. Retreat stays range in length from a short 9–4 mini day, to a week or longer. Send for a schedule of upcoming retreats announced in our quarterly newsletter. Spiritual direction is available upon request.

Facilities include a comfortable cedar log retreat house accommodating up to 20 guests in 12 single and 4 double rooms. Linens and towels are furnished. A Chapel, library, book nook, large and small meeting areas, and many quiet spaces are conducive to rest and reflection. There are walking and skiing trails, canoes, a screened gazebo, and opportunities to enjoy wildlife in a beautiful natural setting.

ARC is located 50 miles north of Minneapolis/St. Paul, and 8 miles northwest of Cambridge, MN. It is situated in a 73 acre pine and hardwood forest with a spring-fed creek and a nearby undeveloped lake.

Call or write for further information or to make arrangements for a private or group retreat.

SAINT FRANCIS CENTER
Saint Francis Hospitality Services
116 8th Avenue S.E.
Little Falls MN 56345
☎ 612 632 0695 or 2981
Contact: Director of Hospitality

Recognizing the need of non-profit groups for affordable accommodations for meetings, conferences and spiritual and wholistic retreats, and wishing to practice good stewardship in the use of available facilities, the Franciscan Sisters of Little Falls sponsor St. Francis Hospitality Services.

This service is envisioned to serve a number of purposes—primarily to offer a simple and nurturing environment to individuals and non-profit groups with limited financial resources. Additionally, the service provides a meeting place for groups whose goals are humanistic, educational, or service-oriented and are in basic accord with the mission and values of the Franciscan Sisters. Therefore, the Center is inclusive of groups from a variety of faiths and cultural backgrounds, and is committed to promoting non-violence and to serving the economically disadvantaged.

At St. Francis Center, functional, comfortable meeting-rooms are available at reasonable rates. 3 rooms can accommodate 30-40 people each, 1 room can accommodate 100. There is a auditorium for 250 people and overnight housing for up to 53. Food and beverage service is available.

For a nominal fee, guests are welcome to use the facilities of St. Francis Health and Recreation Center. The fitness center has a swimming pool, gym, whirlpool, exercise and weight rooms, tennis courts and sauna. The swimming pool can be rented by large groups, but reservations are necessary. Racquetball courts are also available by reservation.

Therapeutic massage therapists are available by prior appointment—a wonderfully relaxing experience for mind and body.

Personal spiritual direction is also available by appointment. Spiritual Directors are members of the Little Falls Franciscan Sisters who have specialized in giving spiritual direction.

You can find a private, peace-filled environment at the Center's 2 hermitages—winterized log cabins nestled in a pine grove clearing. Each cabin contains a bed, small desk and chair, half bath, small stove and fridge. A hermitage is a structure, simple in nature and design, created to provide solitude outside an institutional setting for an individual to live alone even for an extended time.

People staying in the Hermitage go it alone, doing their own cooking and cleaning. Users are welcome to bring their own food. There is an additional charge if food is provided. The serene setting offers privacy and space, yet provides access to daily Mass and emergency needs. Closeness to nature and private prayer life is very much in keeping with a Franciscan lifestyle which is patterned after the example set by St. Francis of Assisi.

Located on the Motherhouse grounds, the Hermitage shares the Franciscan concept of peace and simplicity and is available for retreats to all persons, regardless of race, religion or way of life. It is handicapped-accessible.

In today's busy, high-pressure world, it is good to get away into the silence of nature. This is very hard for most people to do—to take time out to be quiet, to listen. Alone in nature it becomes easier.

The Center is located on the south side of Little Falls just off Highway 10. Parking is free. Call or write to make reservations and to receive further information.

THE DWELLING PLACE
A Place of Hospitality and Prayer
HC–01 Box 126
Brooksville MS 39739
☎ & FAX 601 738 5348
Contact: Sister Clare Van Lent

The Dwelling Place was founded as a Franciscan Prayer Center in 1987. It consists of 17 acres out in the country. Three hermitages, a chapel, a library, a retreat housing unit for up to 8 people, and an administration building are clustered near a pond and a new pine forest.

The staff is comprised of 4 Franciscan Sisters from Dubuque, Iowa. Sister Clare Van Lent is the administrator and retreat director.

Group Retreats are offered two weekends each month. Maximum capacity is 11 people. The remainder of the days are available for private or individually directed retreats.

Weekend retreats begin at 7PM on Friday and close at 1PM on Sunday. The fee is $38 per day or $75 per weekend. A $25 deposit must accompany registration at least one week prior to the retreat.

Because of its ecumenical nature, more and more people come to find quiet, peace, support and healing at The Dwelling Place. Here a loving God awaits His people for a time of prayer, solitude, direction and healing.

MARIA FONTE SOLITUDE
P.O. Box 322
High Ridge  MO 63049
☎ 314 677 3235
Contact: Retreat Director

QUEEN OF HEAVEN SOLITUDE
Route 1, Box 107A
Marionville  MO 65705
☎ 417 744 2011
Contact: Retreat Director

Retreats are available for a day, a week, a weekend, a month, any time of the year. The Priests, Brothers and Sisters invite you to withdraw from the noise and clutter of everyday life and spend time alone with the Lord.

Solitude is not a luxury, but a near necessity for every Christian from time to time, in order to deepen one's relationship to God, to evaluate one's commitment to Him, and to find wisdom and strength for gospel living.

A separate hermitage complete with linens, shower, toilet, heat and air conditioning is provided for each retreatant on these wooded retreat grounds. Ample areas for walking, praying and reading. Three meals provided and taken privately. A library of books and tapes is available, and Spiritual Direction is available on request. Retreatants are invited to share in the daily celebration of the Mass and Liturgy of the Hours with the religious community.

Strong walking shoes, rainwear, an alarm clock, and a flashlight are recommended. We also suggest bringing a tape recorder and a small coffee pot or immersion rod for boiling water.

Maria Fonte Solitude is near St. Louis. Queen of Heaven Solitude is near Springfield, Missouri. For further information or reservations, write or call the Solitude nearest you.

## PASSIONIST NUNS
15700 Clayton Road
Ellisville MO 63011

This strictly cloistered monastery of Passionist Nuns welcomes all to visit and worship in their public chapel which is open for Holy Mass, Monday-Friday at 6:30AM and Saturday–Sunday at 7:30AM. Exposition of the Blessed Sacrament is on Fridays until 4:30PM.

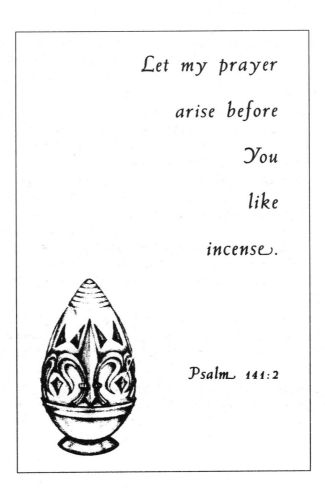

Let my prayer

arise before

You

like

incense.

Psalm 141:2

SAINT LOUIS ABBEY
500 South Mason Road
Saint Louis  MO 63141
☎ 314 434 2557 (Monastery)
   314 434 3412 (Abbot)
Contact: Guestmaster

This small community of Benedictine monks offers hospitality to men who are discerning a call to monastic life, and when space is available, to private retreatants–men only. The few guest rooms are within the monastic enclosure.

Call or write for further information.

FRESH RENEWAL CENTER
P.O. Box 219
Augusta MO 63332
☎ 314 228 4548 or 314 781 1317
Contact: Dick and Cheryl McKinley

Renewal is a retreat with a 12-Step focus offering:
Weekend Renewal Programs
Day-long hospitality seminars
12-Step teaching sessions
Pastoral care and 5th Step process
Inservice for organizations
Outreach to other locations

Dick McKinley is a Certified Specialist in Addiction Medicine (ASAM) and a Certified Chemical Dependency Counselor. He is the founder of Twelve Onward, addressing addictions and damaging dependencies on a Renewal path towards wholeness.

Cheryl McKinley is a graduate of the Clergy Training Program at Hazelden Foundation in Minnesota. She is a Master of Arts in Theology and is a Certified Chemical Dependency Practitioner.

At present, FRESH uses the hospitality of established facilities in St. Louis, as well as the McKinley's house—chalet style on 85 acres overlooking the Missouri River Valley. They are planning Fresh Renewal Center—a continuous live-in center of hospitality and fellowship for 12-Step program participants.

The Renewal Programs are open to all persons in recovery using a 12-Step Program. It is recommended that one have a 6-month 12-Step group attendance by way of background. The basic building blocks are: familiarity with surrender and using your Higher Power; reliance on and faith in group process; and desire to seek the 'more' to which the 12-Step way of life leads and promises.

To share our common experience in a safe setting, to have time to feel for ourselves and know once again that we are not alone—these are the elements of Renewal. To affirm that our Higher Power and the Fellowship and Steps are our strong allies—these are the elements of Renewal.

Reflect on values and the meaning of life

Explore new ways of looking at the world and yourself

Nurture and be nurtured emotionally, intellectually,
physically and spiritually

Empower self and others to live responsible and
constructive lives

Work together to discover life's purpose for you

Accept with renewed commitment the direction provided
by spiritual principles

Love self and others and be loved in return—unselfishly,
humbly and charitably

:  ———————————————————————————————  :

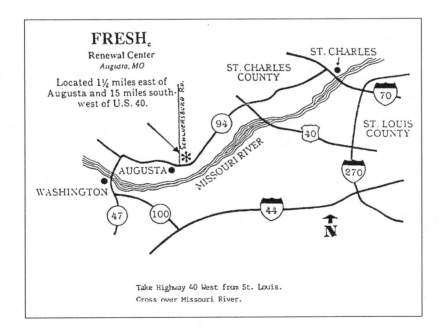

FRESH<sub>e</sub>
Renewal Center
*Augusta, MO*

Located 1½ miles east of
Augusta and 15 miles southwest of U.S. 40.

ST. CHARLES

ST. CHARLES
COUNTY

ST. LOUIS
COUNTY

Take Highway 40 West from St. Louis.
Cross over Missouri River.

SACRED HEART RENEWAL CENTER
P.O. Box 20795
26 Wyoming Ave.
Billings  MT 59104
☎ 406 252 0322
Contact: Bev Gormley, Director

The Sacred Heart Renewal Center offers a four-story building on the grounds of the high school in downtown Billings, once the convent for teachers within the school system. They love people to stay with them for refreshment while journeying across the country, but guests must be on church business, or desiring the peace and quiet within this house of prayer. Regular programs are offered for groups.

There is no live-in staff. Facilities include: a kitchen for guests to use, 34 bedrooms, 2 conference rooms for large groups several smaller group rooms for meetings, a dining room and library. The Chapel seats 60 comfortably.

Write or call for reservations and rates or suggested donation.

SHRINE OF OUR LADY OF GRACE
R.R.1 Box 521
Colebrook NH 03576
☎ 603 237 5511
Contact: Father Director
*The Missionary Oblates of Mary Immaculate*

Sunday Programs take place from Mothers' Day in May to the second Sunday in October at this beautiful place of pilgrimage:

Tour of the Shrine, 1PM
Way of the Cross, 2PM
Main Ceremony, Rosary, Sermon and Benediction, 3PM

Daily Mass is at 11AM.

Food is prepared only for groups on pilgrimage: same selection for all. There are no accommodations, but a list of local lodging places is available on request.

The Oblates of Mary Immaculate was founded in France on January 25th, 1816. The priests and brothers operate shrines all over the world.

Call or write to make reservations for your group. Individuals are welcome to visit during the open season.

## ST. JOSEPH'S VILLA—GUEST & RETREAT HOUSE
Peapack
New Jersey 07977
☎ 908 234 0334
Contact: Directress

Built at the turn of the century, this house is one of the most impressive of the Somerset Hills Mansions. Formerly called 'Blairsden,' it is a 3-storey brick and limestone example of architectural mastery. Since its acquisition by the Sisters of St. John the Baptist, St. Joseph's Villa has been a story of love and a daily miracle of Divine Providence.

Today the chateau with the mountain-top view and landscaped terraces is a place of prayer and meditation for the nuns, and a place of refuge and solace from the pressures of everyday life for hundreds of women who appreciate the seriousness of spiritual progress.

There is a small Chapel and daily Eucharistic celebration, a cheerful dining room with good food, and an elevator. Year-round accommodations: Private room and bath, double and triple rooms with bath, rooms without private bath.

Programs include: Weekend Retreats for women, seminarians and couples; Days of Recollection for men and women; Evenings of Prayer for men and women; Communion Breakfasts for men and women; Private Retreats.

St. Joseph's Villa can accommodate women for 2 nights or more at $50 per day; permanent and temporary residents and those on vacation—please call or write for current rates. Prices include 3 meals a day.

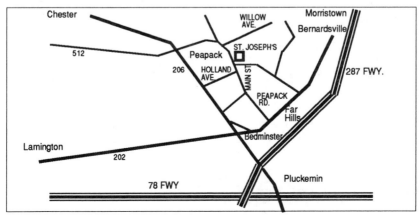

XAVIER CENTER
P.O. Box 211
Convent Station NJ 07961
☎ 201 292 6488
Contact: Arlene M. Kleissler, Director of Marketing

Xavier Center is located on the campus of the College of St. Elizabeth in the town of Convent Station. The campus is 200 acres, safe and scenic, on Route 124, close to Routes 24, 78, 280 and 287. Easy access by car. Public transport by train or bus stops near the campus entrance. 30 minutes from Newark Airport. One hour from New York City.

The Retreat and Conference Center schedules its own programs. It can be rented by non-profit religious, educational and community groups planning, their own programs. Private retreatants and those who wish a Directed Retreat are also welcome.

WORLD APOSTOLATE OF FATIMA
SHRINE OF THE IMMACULATE HEART OF MARY
Mountain View Road
P.O. Box 976
Washington NJ 07882
☎ 908 689 1700
Contact: Pilgrimage Reservations

The Shrine is a permanent reminder of the events of 1917 which came as a salvific medicine to a world so often built without God as the cornerstone. A pilgrimage here, more than offering you more words, talk and mind stimulation, will be an experience, an encounter with the sacred, a time to be in a silence rich with spiritual overtones.

The Oblate Fathers of the Virgin Mary celebrate Holy Mass, hear confessions and give spiritual direction. The Handmaids of Mary Immaculate Sisters serve the Shrine in many ways, including greeting pilgrims and answering questions on the message of Our Lady of Fatima. The sisters reside in the convent adjacent to the Holy House, USA, a replica of the Holy House of Loreto, Italy. According to tradition, the Holy House of Nazareth was transported by angels several times until it finally reached Loreto, Italy in 1294. Today its stands at this same place, enshrined in the magnificent Basilica of Loreto.

The Rosary Garden, with 15 distinct settings depicting the Mysteries of the Rosary, is located in a selected area in the beautiful woodland surrounding the Holy House. Pilgrims are encouraged to make their visit to the Shrine a day of recollection and prayer. There is a dress code.

Limited accommodation is available at Marian Manor, 15 minutes away. Contact Rosemary Dunn for information: 908 479 6194. There are restaurants, motels and hotels in the area. There is a picnic area, and a concession truck is available if requested in advance by a group. Write or call for the group pilgrimage reservation form and a detailed description of the Shrine.

*Scripture itself invites us to interpret pilgrimage in this way. It presents pilgrimage to a sanctuary as a decisive point in one's spiritual life (Deut.16:16), as a joyous community experience (Ps.84:122) in which Jesus, too, participated annually with His parents (Lk.2:41-42). It leads one before the Lord, to seek His face, to experience the joy of His house, which prefigures that eschatalogical day when one will enjoy unending happiness in the beatific vision.*
—Pope John Paul II

DOMINICAN RETREAT HOUSE
Our Lady Queen of Peace
5825 Coors Rd. S.W.
Albuquerque NM 87121
☎ 505-877-4211
Contact: The Guestsister

The Dominican Retreat House offers Spiritual Retreats: Guidance or Direction by staff members, $10-$15 per session.

There are year-round accommodations for 36 overnight guests in 31 rooms. Four hermitages occupy one building in a wide expanse of desert land. Retreatants prepare their own breakfast and lunch, dinner is served daily. Cost: $35 per day. The rate for Weekend Retreats is $60. There is a variety of programs open to men and women.

The Retreat is situated on 70 acres of New Mexico Desert with a view of the Sandia and the Manzano Mountains. There is a small desert chapel near the hermitage. Sturdy walking shoes are a must.

Call or write for further information.

GHOST RANCH CONFERENCE CENTER
HC77, Box 11
Abiquiu NM 87510
☎ 505 685 4333
FAX 505 685 4519
Contact: Ghost Ranch Registrar
*Sponsored by the Presbyterian Church (USA)*

During the year, space not required for program participants is made available for the rest and relaxation of individuals and families. Hiking trails are open, the library is available, and many interesting cultural and historical and recreational sites are within an easy day's trip. Ghost Ranch is set in the quiet, serene and awe-inspiring landscape of the high desert.

During the summer, space is not confirmed until four weeks prior to requested dates.

Ghost Ranch Service Corps: throughout summer, participants work 5 hours a day at a variety of tasks that help run the Ranch and its ministry. This is recommended for people familiar with the Ranch. —No registration fee, room and board half-price. Further information will be sent with confirmation of registration.

No pets or radio/tape players without earphones. The Ranch is equipped to meet the needs of handicapped people, make note of requirements on the registration form. Limited scholarships are available on basis of need.

Winter/spring Housing: most rooms are double occupancy with shared bath. Bedding and towels are provided. Single rooms: $6 surcharge as available. Room and board: $40 per day or $38 after June 1st. Children 12 and under, half-price; 3 and under, free.

There is no activity program for children, and no resident nurse during the winter/spring session. The swimming pool, cantina and horse-riding concession operate only in summer.

Meals: Breakfast $5, Lunch $6, Dinner $6.50. Children 12 and under, half-price; 3 and under, free.

Alternative housing is available after mid-May in casitas (bunkhouses). Bring your own sleeping bag/bedding and towels. $27 per day, including meals. Children 12 and under, half-price; 3 and under, free.

The registration fee listed for each event must accompany your registration form, and is refundable up to one month before the event, less $15 processing fee. Room and board charges are paid on arrival. Credit cards are not accepted.

A full schedule of seminar events and Elderhostels takes place from January 1st to December 1st each year. Write or call for the current program brochure. Ghost Ranch is also available for individual retreats and meetings and events planned by other groups on a space-available basis.

Ghost Ranch is northwest of Santa Fe, 40 miles beyond Espanola on U.S. Highway 84. Transportation to the Ranch is arranged from the Albuquerque or Santa Fe bus station or train depot. Ask for details. Failure to cancel van reservations if you change travel plans, incurs $10 charge.

An education and mission facility of the Presbyterian Church since 1990, the Ranch was given to the church by Arthur and Phoebe Pack in 1955. The Director of Ghost Ranch is a member of the Presbyterian national staff.

PLAZA RESOLANA EN SANTA FE
STUDY & CONFERENCE CENTER
401 Old Taos Highway
Santa Fe  NM 87501
☎ 505 982 8539

*La Resolana* is the northern wall of the plaza that receives the warm afternoon rays of the winter sun. Plaza Resolana is a place of community life where people meet to exchange ideas and news—a comfortable place for individual rest and retreat. There are community-based programs, artists and scholars in residence, seminar programs for individuals in the areas of Inter-American Reconciliation, Leadership Development, Faith, Art, Human Spirituality, and Cross Cultural Understanding.

Facilities include comfortable and affordable meeting space particularly for the religious and educational community; Elderhostels; and rooms for over 70 people, double occupancy, half baths, shared showers and tubs. Pay phone, laundry. Meals are not provided.

Overnight accommodations are on a space-available basis. Reservations are taken no earlier than 30 days prior to your visit. Single–$49, Double–$57. Two-bedroom apartment for 3-5 people–$75 per day.

Plaza Resolana en Santa Fe is 1 hour north of Albuquerque. It occupies the site of the historic Allison-James Mission School, 7000 feet above sea-level.

## MADONNA RETREAT CENTER
4000 St. Joseph's Place N.W.
Albuquerque NM 87120
☎ 505 831 8196
Contact: Tom Schellenbach, Director, or Sister Virginia Lovato SC

If space is available, a non-directed Private Retreat may be made when a Group Retreat is taking place. Meals are provided when a Group Retreat is in session. At other times private retreatants take meals at local eateries.

The Madonna Retreat Center can accommodate 100 people in 50 comfortable rooms, 8 with private baths—others use semi-private or shared common facilities: Single beds, conference rooms, deck, lounge. A laundry/dry-cleaning service is available. No televisions or phones in bedrooms. The cafeteria seats 250, food service is handled through the Center—approved caterer only. Doors are locked at 10PM and open at 7AM.

1994 Rates:

| | |
|---|---|
| Double occupancy | $18 per person/night without bath |
| | $23 with semi-private bath |
| | $25 with private bath |
| Single occupancy | $23 per person/night without bath |
| | $35 with semi-private bath |
| | $40 with private bath |

Prices are subject to change.

Reservations are confirmed with a deposit of $10 per person/night, cancellation refunds only with 60 days notice. The deposit is non-refundable during peak months: February, March, April, June, July, and October.

The Madonna Retreat Center rests on top of the West Mesa in Albuquerque, and has a panoramic view of the Sandia Mountains, the Rio Grande, the city below, and enjoys spectacular southwest sunrises and sunsets. It is 8 miles from downtown, and is surrounded by acres of mystical landscape. The Center is open year-round. Call or write for further information.

MONASTERY OF CHRIST IN THE DESERT
Abiquiu NM 87510
*No phone. Answering service only.*
Contact: Brother Andre Lemieux, Guestmaster.


The Monastery provides for Spiritual Retreats of more than one night. Guests are encouraged to take part in the common prayer, meals, and the work of the monastery on at least some days. All meals are taken *in convento* in the monastic refectory. No red meat is eaten.

$25 per day covers guest's expenses. Hot and cold water in bathrooms. Kerosene lamps. Wood stove in each room.

There is no public transportation to the monastery, which has a 13-mile driveway: Forest Service Road 151—winding, steep and narrow, dirt and clay, slippery when wet. The rainy season is during July and August. Situated at 6500-foot level, there are hiking areas around the monastery.

The closest airport is in Albuquerque, 135 miles away. The monastery is 75 miles north of Santa Fe, and 53 miles south of Chama, off Route 84.

Write well in advance for reservations, and allow several weeks for a reply as the monastery is so isolated.

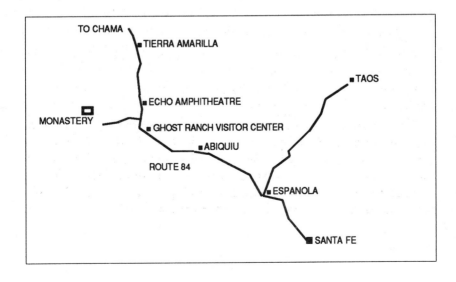

ABBEY OF THE GENESEE
P.O. Box 900
Piffard NY 14533
☎ 716 243 2220
Contact: Guestmaster

The Trappists at the Abbey of the Genesee offer serious monastic retreats, retreatants must remain on the grounds. There are three retreat houses. Meals are taken at Bethlehem House. Self-catering Semi-private Retreats are provided in Bethany House and Cana House (except June through September).

If possible, book 3 months in advance, but reservations can be made at any time.

The Abbey is located on the western slope of the Genesee River Valley in western New York State. The hamlet of Piffard is 4 miles west of Genesee, 35 miles south of Rochester and 55 miles east of Buffalo.

BEAVER CAMP
Star Route, Box 221
Lowville NY 13367
☎ 315 376 2640 *Camp*
315 346 6006 *Residence*
Contact: Eric Buzzell, Program Director

The Adirondack Mennonite Camping Association offers Group and Private Retreats at affordable rates.

Beaver Camp is a year-round Christian Camp and Retreat Center on Beaver Lake in the Adirondack foothills of upstate New York. It is Christ-centered, with the primary emphasis on Christian Summer Youth Camps. Renting the facilities to guest groups is another vital part of the Camp's ministry, as well as the Cherith Program for personal retreats.

The Cherith Program is guided Personal Retreat, the amount of involvement with the guide is determined by the retreatant during the orientation. The usual range for a private retreat is from 1-7 days, private, comfortable and cozy motel units are provided. Meals may be available in the lodge, or self-catered.

The facilities include rustic cabins and modern motel units, a turn-of-the-century Main Lodge where home-cooked meals are provided. There are outdoor activities throughout the year. Beaver Camp is set in 90 acres of unspoiled beauty and serenity. It is about 20 miles from Lowville.

1994 Rates:

| | |
|---|---|
| One day | $22 |
| One night | $38 (from 9AM first day to 9PM second day) |
| Additional nights | $32 |
| Bedding/Towels | $6 |

Add 10% for Friday and Saturday reservations.

Meals in the Lodge:

| | |
|---|---|
| Breakfast | $3.50 |
| Lunch | $5.50 |
| Dinner | $7.00 |

Write or call for further information and reservations.

BEAVER FARM RETREAT AND CONFERENCE CENTER
Corner of Underhill Avenue and Route 118
Yorktown Heights  NY 10598
☎ 914 962 6033
Contact: Nonnie C. Braddock

The Beaver Farm Retreat is an Ecumenical Interfaith Center, providing Group and Private Retreats.

In the 1920s it was a large dairy farm, on 13 acres with a pond. The Victorian mansion can accommodate 38 overnight guests. Larger day groups are easily accommodated. Some of the older outbuildings have been converted to charming meeting rooms, and these are available to groups for additional fees.

1994 Rates:

Shared room and bath, linens and towels provided: $29 per person/night. $5 per person/day facility use fee.

Meals are taken buffet style:

| | |
|---|---|
| Breakfast | $5 |
| Lunch | $8 |
| Dinner | $11 |
| Beverages | $1 |
| Snacks | $2/$3 |

Retreatants assist in clean-up. Special dietary needs can be accommodated with advance notice.

Call or write for reservations.

**ABBA HOUSE OF PRAYER**
647 Western Avenue
Albany NY 12203
☎ 578 438 8320
Contact: Sr. Elizabeth Hoye RSCJ *or* Sr. Mary Gen Smyth RSCJ

*Purposes and Goals:*

To be a true center of prayer, by which we mean praise and worship of God, and active intercession for the dioceses, the church and the world.

To be an open contemplative house where persons from all walks of life can come to grow in their own prayerfulness by experiencing the support of a praying, welcoming community.

To instruct others in prayer and in the study of the Scriptures, by offering the atmosphere supportive of private retreats, the skills necessary to give directed retreats, and various specific ongoing programs such as Bible Classes, Days of Recollection, Talks on Prayer, Spiritual Counselling, etc.

To serve outside the house in various parishes, giving Bible Classes, Days of Retreat, Talks on Prayer, etc.

To pray for Christian Unity and to witness to it by frequent contacts with people of other denominations in mutual love and service.

To be a source of consciousness-raising for the advancement of justice and peace in this world, through all the above means.

✠

Abba House of Prayer is a place apart where one can stop and pray awhile in the chapel for a few hours during the day or evening, for a day, overnight, a weekend or for a few days, for rest and rejuvenation. Private and Directed Retreats. Spiritual guidance with a trained member of staff is available on request. Daily Eucharist is celebrated at noon or towards evening in the house or at a local parish. The staff prays together twice a day: in early afternoon and after dinner.

Abba House caters to Spiritual Sabbaticals lasting from 1–11 months. Call or write for complete details. 2 or 3 Sabbaticals and 2 or 3 retreatants can be accommodated at a given time.

116

Facilities include a quiet family-style atmosphere, 6 guest rooms, a chapel, library, and large enclosed yard. The evening meal is taken together. The House is set in an attractive urban residential neighborhood which is good for walks.

Weekly scripture classes, group retreats, short series on various topics, and prayer experiences are all offered. Other programs may be available on request. Call or write for further information and to make arrangements. With advance notice, we can pick up visitors at bus, train or airline terminals.

A donation of $30 for overnight visitors, $60 for weekend visitors is asked. A donation is appreciated for part of a day, and for Spiritual Direction.

BETHANY RETREAT HOUSE
County Road 105
P.O. Box 1003
Highland Mills NY 10930
☎ 914 928 2213
Contact: Agnes Desautels RJM

Bethany Retreat House is conducted by the Religious of Jesus and Mary, offering Private, Directed and Group Retreats. It is open year-round for a variety of retreats for the individual and groups.

The Cottage and Hermitage is available for a special taste of solitude. Bethany sleeps 25-30 in 27 bedrooms. We serve up to 80 for day programs. Meals are provided. There is a large chapel and a smaller Blessed Sacrament prayer room.

The property borders a small lake at the foot of the Catskill Mountains, and abounds in the beauties of nature, conducive to prayer and reflection. There are plenty of opportunities for walks in wooded terrain. Boating and swimming in the lake are possible at certain times of the year.

Bethany Retreat House is 50 miles from the north of New York City. Pick-up is possible if arranged beforehand, from the bus stations at Highland Mills or Monroe, which are served by the Short Line bus.

A non-refundable deposit is applied to the total cost. For further information regarding costs, reservations and directions, contact the secretary.

THE MERCY PRAYER CENTER
65 Highland Avenue
Rochester NY 14620
☎ 716 473 6893
Contact: Sister Therese Richardson RSM

The Mercy Prayer Center is a small retreat house run by the Sisters of Mercy. It is a quiet place with beautiful grounds and a small chapel. 8 guests can be accommodated in comfortable, private rooms.

Call or write for further information and reservations.

CONVENT OF SAINT HELENA
Box 426
Vails Gate  NY 12584
☎ 914 562 0592
Contact: Guest Team Member

This Episcopal Convent and Guest House welcomes guests for Private Retreats or scheduled Conducted Retreats. Spiritual Direction is available.

Guests share meals with the Sisters and are invited to join them for daily Eucharist and the Monastic Office four times a day. The chapel is open at all times. There is a fine library, and walking trails are available to guests.

The Convent of St. Helena is set on 50 acres, 60 miles north of New York City. There is regular bus service from the City. Suggested donation for private room and 3 meals: $40-45 per day.

CHAPEL HOUSE
Colgate University
13 Oak Drive
Hamilton NY 13346
☎ 315 824 7675
Contact: Director, Chapel House

Opened in 1959–a gift from an anonymous donor–Chapel House provides for Private Retreats, overnight or day use. It is built on a hill in the woods above Colgate University, affording solitary walks through the woodlands and fields of delightful plant-life.

There are 7 simply-furnished rooms with private baths. Facilities include a library, works of religious art, a music room, serene chapel, and a dining room.

Breakfast–self-serve:    8-10AM
Dinner:    12:30PM
Supper:    6PM

Tea or coffee is available in the kitchen. No food or beverages may be taken beyond the dining room.

The usual stay is a minimum of two nights. While here, guests are asked not to visit the campus or village. In order to protect the privacy of others, no visitors are allowed whilst in residence. Conversation only at mealtimes. Phones for emergency use only. Restricted smoking area. No alcohol or drugs. The House is locked from 10:30PM to 8AM.

Ecumenical, in the global sense, the Self-directed Retreat at Chapel House is for anyone who takes the initiative to seek religion's insight and understanding, by using the books, records, works of art, Chapel and privacy and quiet provided here.

The Chapel has been reserved periodically by various religious denominations for services, and Quaker services are held regularly on Sunday mornings. Make reservations several days in advance. Also available for group celebrations.

Current rate: $20 per night, including room and board.

Hamilton is located on Route 12B.

SHRINE OF OUR LADY OF THE ISLAND
Montfort Missionaries
P.O. Box 26
Eastport, Long Island NY 11941

Masses:
Monday–Saturday 9:30AM in the Chapel
Sunday and Holy Days, 10AM.

The founder of the Montfort Missionaries, Saint Louis–Marie Grignon de Montfort (1673–1716) was an itinerant preacher, and a tireless pilgrim for God alone. These missionaries are 'people persons' as he was, and as the Daughters of Wisdom, the women's congregation he and Marie–Louise Trichet founded. They are passionately in love with a 'people God'. There are approximately 1200 priests and brothers worldwide in 36 countries.

There are no accommodations at the Shrine, but there is a Holiday Inn 10 miles west of the Shrine, in Shirley, NY.

Write for further information.

## NATIONAL SHRINE OF THE NORTH AMERICAN MARTYRS
Auriesville NY 12016

*Under the direction of the Jesuits of the New York Province.*

North American Martyrs Shrine began in 1885 as a monument to these first saints of North America to be canonized. The various outdoor shrines and the unique Coliseum Church remind us that this hallowed ground is sanctified by the blood of zealous followers of Christ.

The Shrine is located in the beautiful Mohawk Valley in eastern New York State, 40 miles west of Albany. There are motels within 3–10 miles of the Shrine.

Also on the same grounds is a Jesuit Retreat House which affords Preached, Directed and Private Spiritual Retreats.

Write for a schedule of activities.

Another Shrine, the National Tekakwitha Shrine, is 4 miles away on Route 5, west of Fonda.

SAINT CABRINI SHRINE
Missionary Sisters of the Sacred Heart
701 Fort Washington Avenue
New York NY 10040
☎ 212 923 3536
Contact: Ms. Debra Stumpf, Shrine Administrator

The St. Cabrini Chapel houses the remains of St. Cabrini, Patron Saint of Immigrants. Novena Services are held here, and a Spanish Mass every month. There is a gift shop. Located in North Manhattan, 10 blocks from the George Washington Bridge, overlooking the tranquil banks of the Hudson and New Jersey.

In manicured grounds, the park-like setting was discovered by St. Cabrini in 1889 as she drove her horse and buggy to what was then the remote northwest edge of NYC, where were only villas of the very rich. She purchased the present property and opened Sacred Heart Villa, a residential school for young ladies. The Saint often stopped and rested here during her worldwide travels in the exhausting task of establishing many schools, hospitals and other institutions.

"Not to the East, but to the West" was the counsel of Pope Leo XIII when he urged St. Cabrini to turn from her original goal of China to the mission of helping Italian immigrants flocking to America at the end of the nineteenth century.

St. Cabrini died in December, 1917 in Chicago, and was buried in West Park, NY. Her body was brought to the School Chapel in 1933. In December 1959, St. Cabrini's body was transferred from the Chapel, to the new, beautiful altar where she now rests enclosed in a glass coffin.

The Chapel provides a video on the life of St. Cabrini as well as a lecture and tour for all groups. Her feast-day is November 13th, when a special celebration at the Chapel includes Masses in English, Italian, Spanish, Filipino and Haitian. The Chapel is open Tuesday through Sunday. The Blessed Sacrament is reserved in an adjoining chapel for those who wish to pray privately. A full or half-day retreat may be scheduled, and there is ample space for quiet prayer and reflection. Mass is celebrated daily.

There are restrooms at the Shrine, but no eating facilities. Visitors may picnic on the lovely grounds. Hospitality for groups: coffee and cake. Fort Tryon Park is a 5-minute walk, and picnickers are welcome there. Eateries and hotels are in the area.

# FRANCISCAN RETREAT CENTER
St. Anthony–on–Hudson
517 Washington Avenue
Rensselaer NY 12144
☎ 518 434 4625 *or* 434 8200
Contact: Brother James M. Moore OFM Conv., Director

The Franciscan Retreat Center, sponsored by Conventual Franciscan Friars, is a 61-bed retreat facility. It is based on the charism of St. Francis of Assisi, and his love for prayer and solitude. It is available for Private Retreats, Conferences, and Workshops of a spiritual/educational nature.

Men and women can be accommodated for a day, weekend, or weeks' experience of prayer. There are 2 beautiful chapels, 2 large conference rooms, 8 small conference rooms, and a dining room. A limited number of double rooms are available. All spaces are accessible to the physically challenged.

*Private Retreats:* $35/day donation. Free to structure own time according to personal needs. Time out from daily routine to reflect on God's initiative in your life. Many areas suitable for praying, meditating, listening, walking or relaxing. Welcome anytime.

*Directed Retreats:* $40/day donation. 1:1 relationship, meet daily with director to share prayer experience based on Scripture, Franciscan sources, etc. Retreatants gather daily for Eucharist and Evening Prayer.

*Preached Retreats:* (Group Retreat) $35/day donation. A series of daily conferences. In the reflective atmosphere of the Center, retreatants are invited to personalize the theme of the day's conference and Eucharist.

*Guided Retreats:* $40/day donation. Similar to Preached Retreats.

Reservations for all retreats will be confirmed upon receipt of a $50 deposit, which is non-refundable but transferable.

The Franciscan Retreat Center is located on 75 acres of high open ground above the east bank of the Hudson River. An atmosphere of peace and solitude prevails, just minutes from downtown Albany. It is at the crossroads of NYC, Boston, Montreal and Syracuse, just off Interstate 90 at exit 7.

Write or call for additional information and program schedule.

## LITTLE PORTION FRIARY
P.O. Box 399
Mount Sinai  NY 11766
☎ 516 473 0553
Contact: The Guestmaster
*The Society of Saint Francis–Anglican*
*The Poor Clares–Semi-cloistered Sisters*

Little Portion Friary provides a serene atmosphere for reflection and renewal–a time to be still and wait upon the Lord. All people of all faiths who seek God or a deeper knowledge of God in their lives, are welcome.

Silence is observed during specified times and all are asked to comply. All are welcome to attend the celebration of a four-fold Daily Office and Eucharist. The Chapel is open all day.

The library in the friary is available to guests, and a Conference Room is open to groups. Brothers are available, on advance notice, to conduct retreats for groups. Speak with the Guestmaster when booking. Arrangements can be made to meet with one of the Brothers for Spiritual Direction and/or the Sacrament of Reconciliation or the Laying on of Hands.

The Little Portion Friary is open to guests Tuesday through Sunday. Individuals are welcome during the week and on weekends as space allows. Group retreats are usually scheduled for weekends.

Suggested donation (subject to change):

| | |
|---|---|
| Group Retreat: | $110/person–2 nights, 5 meals |
| | $60/person–1 night, 3 meals |
| Individuals: | $50 per night, 3 meals |

Make reservations in advance. A 50% non-refundable deposit is required to reserve the Guesthouse for a Group Retreat. No deposit is required for Individual Retreats.

*Wayside House* accommodates 16 people in 3 double rooms and the rest in single rooms. There are 3 baths with showers, a kitchenette and parlor on the main floor. Extra bedrooms are sometimes available in the Friary. Check with the Guestmaster. No cooking in the Guesthouse, all meals are taken with the Community in the Friary dining room.

*Little Portion Friary* is situated on 20 acres, mostly wooded. Guests are free to walk the grounds and use the outdoor Chapel. The Friary is approximately 60 miles east of NYC, on the north shore of Long Island, minutes from the beach and local shopping, near Point Jefferson of the Long Island Railroad. If possible, a Brother will meet the train; otherwise taxis are available. Point Jefferson–Bridgeport Ferry is also convenient.

In keeping with Franciscan tradition, the Brothers bake bread once a week, for sale in the Bake Shop Friday to Sunday. The Gift Shop is open daily.

*May the Lord Bless you and protect you.*
*May He show you His countenance and have mercy on you.*
*May He turn His face to you and give you peace.*
*May the Lord bless you.*

–St. Francis

———

MOUNT SAINT FRANCIS HERMITAGE
Conventual Franciscan Friars
P.O.Box 276
Maine  NY 13802
☎ 607 754 9813
Contact: The Director

Mount St. Francis is a place of solitude, where one may enter the wilderness of God alone through prayer, silence and retreat.

Call for suggested donation and reservations.

OUR LADY'S GUEST AND RETREAT HOUSE
Route 1, Box 163B
Garrison NY 10524
☎ 914 424 3300
Contact: Sister Ita Flynn SA

Our Lady's Guest and Retreat House, with its atmosphere of solitude and prayer, is a place of spiritual refreshment.

The Franciscan Sisters of the Atonement believe Graymoor is a special place of peace and blessing. It was here the Society of the Atonement was founded in 1898, and it is to Graymoor that their missionaries return to renew contact with their roots, their history and their charism, before departing for missions throughout the world. Here, the Franciscan way of life, a blending of prayer and work, is lived daily.

The Sisters, in Franciscan hospitality, invite retreatants to experience this atmosphere of peace and blessing, away from the concerns of home, to rest and reflect and listen to the presence of God in their lives.

Renewed in body and spirit, many have found the courage and confidence they need to return to the obligations and demands of their daily lives. COME AND PRAY!

Weekend Retreats are usually reserved for specialized groups. Private Retreats are by arrangement. Our Lady's Guest and Retreat House also sponsors Pilgrimage Days and Days of Recollection.

Call or write for complete information and current rates.

RESURRECTION HOUSE
20 River Street
Saranac Lake NY 12983
☎ 518 891 1182
Contact: Sister Rita Mawn OCDS

Set on Lake Flower in the Adirondack Mountains, Resurrection House, a Carmelite Monastery, provides for Private and Group Retreats and the Hermitage Experience.

Mass is celebrated at 7:30AM, and Evening Prayer in the Chapel. The parish church (next door) offers services too. The following are available to guests:

    Charismatic Prayer Group
    Morning Meditation Group
    Healing Prayer Team
    Spiritual Guidance
    Fasting or shared meals
    Various recreations: walking, skiing, swimming etc.

Facilities include 8 single rooms for private retreatants. For groups there are 3 double beds, 6 singles, or room for 20 people with sleeping bags. Groups may cook for themselves and provide for their own program. There is an extensive book and tape library.

Cost per person: $15/night; $5/day for hermitage; $75/week; $150/month.

Call or write for reservations.

## SAINT MARY'S CONVENT
John Street
Peekskill NY 10566
☎ 914 737 0113
Contact: Guest Mistress

The Episcopal Community of Saint Mary was founded in New York City in 1865. The Sisters live a monastic life centered on the daily Eucharist and a five-fold Divine Office. The Altar Bread Department at the Convent serves parishes, shipping over 12 million wafers each year. Retreatants are invited to participate in some way in the Sisters' prayer life. The Guest Mistress is available if one wishes to talk with someone.

*St. Benedict's House* is a split-level, modern building with 18 single rooms, 1 efficiency apartment with twin beds, a library and bookstore.

*St. Gabriel's House* has a conference room and a few rooms for individual guests.

All meals are taken at the Convent, mostly in silence.

There is a $10 non-refundable deposit for Conducted Retreats. The suggested donation for a Conducted Retreat is $75 per weekend with 6 meals; $35 for overnight guests with meals. Snacks are available in the kitchen. Basics for breakfast are available for those who sleep late. With advance notice, special dietary needs can be met. No smoking indoors.

Call or write for reservations.

## TRANSFIGURATION MONASTERY
701 New York Route 79
Windsor NY 13865
☎ 607 655 2366
Contact: Sister Jeanne Marie Pearse OSB

The Transfiguration Monastery is a small contemplative monastic community following the Rule of St. Benedict in a daily rhythm of prayer, work and study. The Monastery stresses classic Benedictine values such as silence, manual work, and reception of guests. The Monastery is also committed to ecologically sound forms of shelter, livelihood and nourishment.

The Monastery is located on 125 acres in Susquehanna Valley, 15 miles east of Binghamton and 165 miles west of New York City. The village of Windsor is nearby. Surrounded by high hills, the Monastery is apart from the noise and pressure of modern society. There are miles of beautiful walks, in the valley or in the woods, on the hills and trails. Country clothing and shoes are advised. Be prepared for all kinds of weather.

The Guesthouse is a place of prayer and quiet for those who need a time apart from their usual responsibilities and occupations. It is small: 4 single rooms and one double. A sitting room can be used as a bedroom when needed. Retreatants make their own schedules except for the noon and evening meals. Breakfast is self-serve, the noon meal is served in the monastery refectory, the evening meal in the Guesthouse.

The Community prays four times a day—all are welcome. Spiritual books are available.

Guests are welcome for stays of a few hours to one week. Reservations must be made in advance. Transportation to and from the bus or airport is available, an offering of $10 each way is suggested. At present, the suggested donation for guests is in the range of $25–$35 per day.

## MOUNT SAVIOUR MONASTERY
Pine City NY 14871
☎ 607 734 1688
Contact: Guestmaster

Mount Saviour Monastery provides Private Retreats for those wanting time apart. Guests structure their own time and may join the Benedictine monks in their work and prayer.

The Monastery is situated on 1000 acres. The monks raise sheep, market lambs, yarn and pelt products. There is a book and gift shop.

Men are accommodated at St. Joseph's Guest House—15 rooms, and meals are taken with the monks. Women and couples are accommodated at 2 Guest Houses: St. Gertrude's—2 double beds, 4 singles; and St. Peter's, a small stone farmhouse which sleeps 2 and has a pull-out couch. There are also 2 small cottages that sleep 2 people.

Minimum stay is 2 nights. A donation of $30 per day is suggested, more if you are able.

Call or write for further information.

STILL POINT HOUSE OF PRAYER
Route 423, Box 53
Stillwater NY 12170
☎ 518 587 4967
Contact: Program Directress

Still Point House of Prayer is a Roman Catholic Contemplative Community of God's people, where the micro-Church happens in a holistic, liturgical, monastic life-style.

Secluded, winterized hermitages are available year-round for guests. There are also rooms in the Guest House. Set in 30 acres of woods, gardens, a pond and a Meditation Park.

Guests are welcome to share a common meal, and to stay for a few hours, a few days, or a weekend of silence and solitude. There are opportunities to share in:

> Spiritual companionship
> Holistic day workshops
> Private Retreat
> Directed Retreats (10-30 days)
> Interfaith programs
> Body work
> Guided Meditation
> Holistic counseling
> Weekend Guided Retreats
> Hermitages
> High School Retreats
> Art classes and cultural experiences at SPAC (summer)

Sabbaticals are offered year-round, self-designed or planned with a Director as a holistic program (partial scholarship available). Contact Sylvia Rosell OP for more information.

HOLY TRINITY MONASTERY
7200 Tobes Hill Road
Hornell NY 14843
☎ 607 324 7624
Contact: John Brewster

This Benedictine Monastery of vowed community members is open to men and women, single, married, couples, vowed, celibates, ordained priests, etc.

Private and directed retreats, one to eight days. Meals are provided for retreatants.

Hermit day —self-directed. Guests have use of the grounds and monastery, including a private room. An atmosphere of stillness and solitude offers opportunities for prayer, reading, exploring the outdoors, and rest.

Advance notice is required. Suggested donation: $30 per night.

The feast of St. Benedict is on July 11th.

Liturgy of the Hours:

| Weekdays: | Morning Prayer | 7:45AM |
|---|---|---|
| | Midday Prayer | Noon |
| | Evening Prayer | 6:15PM |
| | Compline | 8:00PM |
| Saturday: | Morning Prayer | 9:00AM |
| Sunday: | Compline | 7:45PM |

Small groups use the monastery for day and evening programs.

HOLY CROSS MONASTERY
(Benedictine Monks –Anglican)
P.O. Box 99
West Park  NY 12493
☎   914 384 6660
FAX 914 384 6031
Contact: The Guesthouse


Planned Group Retreats throughout the year. Meeting-room fees.

Elevator in main building. Non-smoking facility.

Individual Retreats: Tuesday 1:30PM to Sunday. $60 per night, room and meals. The Guesthouse is closed from Sunday evening until Tuesday afternoon.

Holy Cross Monastery is located on Route 9W, West Park, south of Kingston. There are 26 acres, partly wooded, on the Hudson River.

# JESUIT HOUSE OF PRAYER
P.O. Box 7
Hot Springs NC 28743
☎ 704 622 7366
Contact: Rev. Vincent Alagia SJ

The Jesuit House of Prayer offers Private Retreats and Directed Retreats. The Directed Retreat is Scripturally-based and filtered through the tradition of the Ignatian Exercises. The retreatant and director meet once a day to reflect on the prayer experience of the retreatant. Arrangements for a 30-day Ignatian Retreat can be made.

Situated in the scenic mountains of Western North Carolina, the House of Prayer offers a peaceful atmosphere for prayer and reflection.

Accommodations are provided for 15 retreatants, 6 in the main house, 9 in an adjacent building. Retreatants prepare their own breakfast and lunch. Although there is an atmosphere of quiet during the day, the evening meal is community-style and provides for socializing. A silent or private meal can be arranged according to the needs or preference of the retreatant.

The Eucharist is celebrated daily. Night Prayer is celebrated after the evening meal.

For those interested in physical activity, the mountains provide hiking trails and creeks to follow. For those interested in the Hot Springs, the town has mineral baths to enjoy. Clothing is casual. Sturdy walking shoes are recommended for hikers.

Suggested donation for hospitality, room and meals:

| | |
|---|---|
| Private Retreat | $30 per night |
| Directed Retreat | $35 per night |
| 30-day Directed Retreat | $900 per person. |

Except for a few weeks, the House of Prayer is open year-round. Call or write to make inquiries, reservations, and for further information, including weekend group rates.

CHRISTIAN FAMILY CENTER
Marianist Family Ministry Inc.
Route 1, Box 259-F
Holly Ridge NC 28445
☎ 919-328-1584
Contact: Dr. Jim Rider

The Christian Family Center, on the ocean at North Topsail Beach, is open for family and group week and weekend retreats. Private retreats and away days are also possible. The Center provides shelter for the homeless and those in distress when it is not being used for retreats.

*September through May:* arrive for week retreats after 2PM Sunday, and stay until Friday afternoon. Bring twin sheets or sleeping bags and towels. Pillows and blankets are provided. There is no fixed charge, donations are accepted.

*June through August:* $89 for each person over eight years old, $55 under eight. Deposit of $144 with application. Partial scholarships are available. Those who cannot afford the full suggested amount of a family week or weekend are asked to pay what it would cost them at home for food.

Other programs: Family Weekend Retreat; Teen Weekends; Lent—A Time for Change; Windows—Healing and Helping Through Loss. Examples of Summer Family Weeks: Single Parents 6/26—7/1; Hispanic Week 7/3—7/8.

## OUR LADY OF CONSOLATION BASILICA & NATIONAL SHRINE

| | |
|---|---|
| 315 Clay Street | *Overnight Lodging Contact:* |
| Carey OH 43316 | Sr. Joan Froning OSF |
| ☎ 419 396 7107 *or* 396 3355 | St. Anthony Pilgrim House |
| Contact: Pilgrim Director | 321 Clay Street |
| | Carey, OH 43316 |
| | ☎ 419 396 7970 |

The Renewal Center is available for group retreats year-round. Contact the Retreat Director for the current schedule.

The Shrine was established by Fr. Joseph P. Gloden, a native of Luxembourg, at the Mission of Carey, which was attached to his church of St. Nicholas at nearby Frenchtown.

In 1878, Pope Leo XIII established a Confraternity at Carey, similar to that of the mother church in Luxembourg. This firmly established the devotion of Our Lady of Consolation in this country.

The Shrine is open 24 hours a day, a holy and powerful place of prayer for people of faith. This shrine is famous for its many miracles. Masses every day.

During the summer, Franciscan Friars lead pilgrims in the devotions of the Stations of the Cross, stone grottoes marking the Way of the Cross, and several exquisite religious statues.

Devotions to Mary as Consoler of the Afflicted was first expressed by St. Ignatius of Antioch in the 2nd century when he wrote: "Mary, knowing what it is to suffer, is ever ready to administer consolation."

The Shrine Park features 30 acres of lovely grounds, dominated by an imposing marble and granite altar with a golden dome and a giant replica of the image of Our Lady of Consolation on top. It is visible for miles, a beacon for all who come and pray.

Sunday Devotions take place May through October: Rosary Procession through the streets with the image of Our Lady of Consolation. After devotions, pilgrims may have ministers pray with them about their needs, and are able to hold or be touched by a relic of the True Cross.

Call or write for reservations and further information.

BERGAMO CENTER FOR LIFELONG LEARNING
4400 Shakertown Road
Dayton OH 45430
☎ 513 426 2363
Fax 513 426 1090
Contact: Program Manager

MISSION STATEMENT:

Bergamo Center for Lifelong Learning exists to educate people of all ages and from all walks of life to appreciate their full human potential and their social responsibility to the human community.

We provide educational and human services which enhance the physical, intellectual, emotional and faith development of individuals, organizations and communities.

We demonstrate a high level of commitment and professionalism as a skilled staff of conference planners, program leaders, educators, counselors and support personnel. We are dedicated to providing excellent and hospitable service to each of our guests.

We serve a worldwide constituency which uses our human services and meeting and recreational facilities to enhance their learning efforts. Our aesthetic and peaceful campus provides an environment conducive to realizing and responding to social responsibilities to work, family, community and church.

Our challenge is to address unmet, changing and evolving needs of individual and community development in order to advance a more integrated and caring society, We strive to exemplify a vision of personal and social renewal in the spirit of John XXIII, in whose inspiration we are founded.

As a center for lifelong learning, we are sponsored by the Society of Mary (Marianists), an international religious order. We are part of their worldwide educational mission to promote a stewardship of life 'from cradle to grave.'

✠

Private retreats are offered when there are vacancies—single rooms with private bath in Roncalli Center. Meals are available when other groups or individuals are in the building at the same time. Meals are optional. Send for current rates and further information.

Ohio

*Bergamo Center for Lifelong Learning, Continued*

THE RONCALLI CENTER is a modern, motel-like design around a landscaped courtyard. Facilities include: versatile meeting and conference rooms for large and small groups, full air-conditioning, single and double rooms with private baths, overnight accommodations for over 90 people, complete dining facilities, a spacious assembly hall/chapel for large meetings and services, and a large lounge with brick fireplace.

SIEBEN HALL is a recreation center with basketball and volleyball courts, a multi-purpose room and a racquetball court.

BERGAMO/MOUNT ST. JOHN NATURE PRESERVE is an outdoor educational center under the aegis of the Ohio Natural Landmark Program. It comprises 80 acres of woods, marsh and prairie, providing a rare glimpse of the influence of Ohio's glacial history on its natural features and vegetation. The Nature Preserve has become a sanctuary for many forms of wildlife. A nature trail which winds through the woods, marsh, old field and prairie habitats, will be expanded after prairie grasses and forbes become firmly established. The Preserve is open to all guests and the public during daylight hours, at no charge. For additional information about group education tours, faculty tours and lecture/seminars, contact the Coordinator of Recreational Facilities: (513) 426-2363.

## OSAGE MONASTERY
O † M Forest of Peace
8701 West Monastery Road
Sand Springs  OK 74063
☎ 918 245 2734
Contact:  Sister Maureen Truland OSB

The Osage Monastery offers Private and Directed Retreats, for overnight or extended stays. It blends Eastern Ashram living with the monastic tradition of the West.

Benedictine Sisters, lay people –contemplative.

Guests may share in Community life and prayer, or have complete solitude.

There are 6 small hermitages with simple sleeping facilities, bath and shower. No cooking facilities or air-conditioning. No families.

## OUR LADY OF PEACE RETREAT
3600 S.W. 170th Avenue
Beaverton OR 97006
☎ 503 649 7127
Contact: Retreat Directress

Our Lady of Peace Retreat provides for Group Retreats, Directed Retreats and Non-directed Retreats. Retreat House facilities include 57 bedrooms and a Chapel.

Cost: approximately $20 per night.

Meals: Breakfast $3; Lunch $4; Dinner $6. Inform the Sisters if you plan to stay for meals and ask where meals are taken and the times they are served.

The Retreat is located on the Tualatin Valley Highway, (OR#8) 2.5 miles west of the center of Beaverton, 10 miles from Portland.

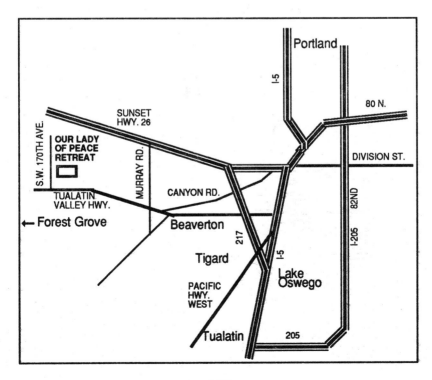

BRIGITTINE MONASTERY OF OUR LADY OF CONSOLATION
The Order of the Most Holy Savior
23300 Walker Lane
Amity OR 97101
☎ 503 835 8080
FAX 503 835 9662
Contact: Guest Brother

The Retreat House can accommodate up to 6 people in private rooms.

The Monastery is located in the midst of the beautiful Willamette Valley, surrounded by trees and farm land. There is a wonderful view of the coastal range mountains.

Call or write for information regarding rates and to make reservations.

## SAINT EMMA MONASTERY AND RETREAT HOUSE
Sisters of Saint Benedict
1001 Harvey Avenue
Greensburg PA 15601
☎ 412 834 3060
Contact: Mother Mary Anne OSB

Saint Emma Monastery offers Retreats for Lay People: Weekend, 5 and 6-day Silent Retreats, Retreats for Married Couples. Individuals are welcome to join these retreats. Also Preached Retreats for Sisters are offered. Individuals are welcome for Private Retreats when space is available during Scheduled Retreats. Protestant groups are welcomed when the calendar permits.

The 1994 weekend fee is $75, including meals. The Retreat House has 54 private rooms, each with a sink.

The Fatima Chapel is provided for retreatants. The Walburga Shrine, in the form of a star, consists of stained-glass windows depicting the life of St. Walburga. Individuals may join the Sisters in the Sacred Heart Chapel for the sung Liturgy of the Hours. There are Stations of the Cross through the orchard, spacious grounds with flower gardens and small shrines. A Crucifixion scene overlooks the Sisters' Cemetery.

The easiest route to the monastery is to take U.S.22 to PA819 (Harvey St.) and head south for 5 miles.

Call or write for further information.

PEACE HERMITAGE
Medical Mission Sisters
8400 Pine Road
Philadelphia PA 19111
☎ 215 342 0961
Contact: Coordinator

Peace Hermitage is an invitation to respond in a special way to the Lord. The hermitage experience provides the space, the silence, the solitude which leads to the discovery of one's own inner truth, a truth we learn best in the wilderness of our own hearts. *I will lead her into the desert and speak to her own heart.*

Hosea 2:16

In solitude, all other voices are stilled. There we listen for the voice of the inner Teacher who leads us to the gift of inner peace. In the midst of the world's noise, turmoil and anxieties, we hear once again the Lord's promise: *My peace I give you...* John 14:27.

The hermitages are located in a grove on the property of the Medical Mission Sisters, and give a sense of seclusion conducive to a prayerful solitude. The property is bordered by two large parks which allow for long walks in the woods, cycling along the creek, or bird-watching. Deer from the wildlife reserve are regular visitors to the hermitages.

The hermitages are single dwellings with their own cooking facilities and heating—available year-round. Guests provide their own food and linens.

People of all religious traditions are welcome. There is opportunity for daily Eucharist in the Sisters' Chapel or in a nearby parish, and a communal evening prayer in the Meditation Chapel, based on the Liturgical Hours of the Catholic tradition. This includes an extended period of prayerful silence.

The Individual Hermitage Experience of Solitude is one of listening to the Spirit who is the real Director of the inner journey. Additional Hermitage Options include: Directed Retreats; Spiritual Companioning; Poustinia; Sabbatical Time; Arts and Spirituality; Wholistic Life-style Retreats.

Working scholarships are available. A non-refundable first-day deposit confirms your reservation. Call or write for further information and current suggested donation.

SPRUCE LAKE RETREAT
R.R. 1, Box 605
Canadensis  PA 18325
☎  717 595 7505
FAX 717 595 0328
Contact: Accommodations Manager
*Owned by: The Franconia Mennonite Camp Assn. Inc.*

Christ ✝ Centered

Spruce Lake Retreat is a year-round Christian retreat center located on 325 acres of quiet woodland, with mountain streams, waterfalls, and two small lakes, wildlife and hiking trails. There is a full range of youth and family programs and lodgings and indoor and outdoor activities. Most recreation is free. Recreation areas are closed during the Sunday morning worship hour. Spruce Lake is also a place where one may go for a personal retreat.

Use of radios, TV, tape players is discouraged, except in your own room or camper where the volume is inaudible outside. No firearms, fireworks, smoking, alcohol or pets. Wildlife is to be left in its natural state. The lobby and recreation areas are closed after 11PM. All areas are quiet after 11PM.

An emergency phone is available at the registration desk in the lobby. There are 2 public phones. Coin-operated clothes-dryer at Pines Lodge. Recycling is encouraged. A Camp nurse is available. The Oak Leaf Book Shoppe sells books, cards, gifts, pottery  and knitwear.

Most sessions programmed by Spruce Lake Retreat are open to anyone at no extra charge, but offerings are taken regularly.

Accommodations: 51 private motel-type rooms with private bath; 8 conference rooms or lounges which can accommodate between 20 and 200 people. 3 group rooms with pianos.

A total of 60 campsites, including sites that may be rented by the season and by the day. Firewood, heated bath-house with showers. Multipurpose Lakeview Program Center. Central dining room, buffet service. Wilderness Area: a self-contained log retreat house sleeping 26. Rustic pavilion with kitchen. Bunkhouse sleeps 36.

Most areas are wheelchair accessible. Spruce Lake Retreat is located 2 hours from New York City, 2.5 hours from Philadelphia, 2.5 miles north of Canadensis on Route 447.

Send for  further details, including current rates for lodging, camping and meals.

BETHEL
Holy Ghost Animation Center
6230 Brush Run Road
Bethel Park  PA 15102
☎ 412 835 3510
Contact: Kathy Lane

Bethel offers Private Retreats, Group Retreats and Conferences. Accommodations: 45 single rooms, each with a twin bed, sink, desk and chair. Community bath/shower room. The facility has large conference rooms, a library, a large dining room and a chapel.

The Center is located on 40 acres of beautiful grounds where deer is often seen.

Call or write in advance for reservations for an overnight retreat or to schedule a longer stay and group retreats. Complete information will be sent on request, including current rates.

## SAINT GABRIEL'S MONASTERY AND RETREAT CENTER
The Passionist Nuns
631 Griffin Pond Road
Clarks Summit  PA 18411
☎ 717 586 4957
Contact: Sister Alene Perry CP

St. Gabriel's Monastery offers Private Retreats at $25 per day, including meals. A $15 non-refundable deposit is required with reservations.

Several other kinds of retreats are accommodated. Spiritual guidance is available, for which a $15 donation is suggested.

*To belong to God*

*and* ∫ *to serve Him*

*in* **Love**

*is the vocation of all.*

Blessed Teresa Benedicta of the Cross
[Edith Stein]

TRINITY SPIRITUAL CENTER
3609 Simpson Ferry Road
Camp Hill  PA 17011
☎ 717 761 7355
Contact: Mary Ann Boyarski Ed.D, Program Director

Trinity Spiritual Center offers varying lengths of stay for Private Retreats, Group Retreats, or for guests seeking a quiet time.

Fee is negotiated at the time of reservation.

The Amish country is about an hour away.

FRANCISCAN SPIRIT AND LIFE CENTER
Grove and McRoberts Roads
Pittsburgh PA 15234
☎ 412 881 9207
Contact: Sister Barbara A Zilch OSF

The Franciscan Spirit and Life Center is available for meetings, seminars and workshops. Day and evening programs are offered. Accommodations include 3 hermitages in a wooded area for days, weekends and weeks of prayer or retreat. Overnight and expanded facilities will be ready in late Spring, 1995.

THE CENACLE
4273 Fifth Avenue
Pittsburgh  PA 15213
☎ 412 681 6180
Contact: Sister Judith Osterburg, Director
*Sisters of the Cenacle*

The Cenacle offers short-stay Private Retreats, Directed Retreats, Group Retreats and Take-Home Retreats.

It is situated in the Oakland area of Pittsburgh, at the corner of Clyde, 2 blocks east of the University of Pittsburgh and St. Paul's Cathedral. Ample parking. Close to buses and airport. Limo pickup 3 blocks away.

Accommodations include 3 single, and 3 double rooms.

Call or write for costs and to make reservations.

REGINA MUNDI PRIORY
Waterloo and Fairfield Roads
Devon PA 19333
Contact: Sister M. Rita, Prioress or Guest Mistress
*Congregation of the Sisters of Jesus Crucified O.S.B.*

Accommodations are provided in a small cottage near the Priory. It has 6 beds in 3 rooms, a kitchenette and dining room. Guests do their own cooking or eat out. Food is provided.

Guests are free to join the Sisters in Mass every day, and in singing the Office 5 times a day.

There are no buses in Devon.

Suggested donation of $15–$20 per day.

LAURELVILLE MENNONITE CHURCH CENTER
Route 5
Mount Pleasant PA 15666
☎ 412 423 2056

The Laurelville Center provides for Private and Group Retreats.

There is a wide range of accommodation. The rates given are for stays of 3 nights with 6 meals:

| | |
|---|---|
| Cabins | $96 |
| Cottages | $129 |
| Lodge | $142 |
| Motel | $154 |
| Guesthouse/Solarhouse | $172 |

The rate for the Guesthouse is $57 per night.

The best time to stay at the Center is September through May, weekdays for 1 to 5 nights. Campsites are also available.

Recreational facilities include: trails through 180 acres in the Laurel Mountains; swimming pool; tennis, volleyball and basketball courts; shuffleboard and miniature golf.

BETHANY RETREAT CENTER
P.O. Box 129
Frenchville PA 16836
☎ 814 263 4855 *or* 814 263 4177
Contact: Director

Bethany Retreat Center is a quiet place to come to be renewed, to pray, and to experience God. Bethany has private and semi-private rooms to accommodate up to 35 people. The spacious dining room can seat up to 100, and looks out over the beautiful countryside. The chapel and the surrounding grounds provide a peaceful atmosphere for prayer and reflection. VCR equipment, audiocassette tapes of various spiritual talks and retreats, a library, and a bookstore are available to retreatants. Home cooked, simple meals.

Group and individual retreats can be arranged. The Center is also available to groups for their own retreats, conferences or meetings.

It is possible to make a private, directed or non-directed retreat, to attend liturgies, and to enjoy the facilities of Bethany Retreat Center with or without individual direction. All retreats are made in an atmosphere of silence.

*Spiritual Direction:* If you are interested in on-going spiritual direction, call Bethany Retreat Center for more information and to make arrangements.

The Center is located on 130 acres of rolling hills and wooded countryside, 15 miles from Interstate 80 (Exit 19).

Call or write for a calendar of events and current rates. All deposits are non-refundable.

OLMSTED MANOR
Box 8
Ludlow PA 16333
☎ 814 945 6512
Contact: Judy

Operated by The United Methodist Church, Olmsted Manor is situated in Pennsylvania's Allegheny National Forest. It is an adult retreat and renewal center, for couples or individuals on private retreat. All denominations may use the facilities, 75% of guests are Methodist. The Tudor-style mansion was built in 1916 and given to the Methodist Church by the Olmsted family in 1969.

Features include spring water, 325 acres, sunken gardens, lily ponds, cascading fountains, terraced flower gardens, a carriage house, picnic grove, putting green, stone fireplace and gazebo. Accommodations are in the Manor and in the motel-style Groves Lodge. It is an elegant facility. Two rooms are at entrance-level, and baths have support bars. Parking lots. Walking and hiking in the National Forest.

Meals are family-style. Special diets can be accommodated if requested on reservation. Refrigerators are available in the Manor and Lodge for medicine storage. Arrangements may be made with staff for limited use of the kitchen.

Groves Lodge accommodates 30. The Manor accommodates 15. The Carriage House, an apartment over former garage, sleeps 4 in 2 bedrooms, it has a living-room, kitchen and bathroom. Rent by the day or week.

Olmsted Manor is open year-round. Fall and the weekends are the busiest times. Bookings fill fast for the summer months too. Mid-week placements are easiest.

Enquire about current rates. A deposit is required, returned if 90-days notification of cancellation is given.

The Center is located on the north side of U.S. Route 6, 90 miles from Erie, PA; 150 miles from Pittsburgh; 110 miles from Buffalo, NY. U.S. Air serves Bradford, PA Regional Airport. Olmsted Manor will provide transportation from there for a small fee.

Our Lord does not consider
the greatness of our works
but the *Love*
with which we do them.

Saint Teresa of Jesus

# NAZARETH SPIRITUAL ENRICHMENT CENTER
12 Cliff Terrace
Newport RI 02840
☎ 401 847 1654
Contact: Registrar and Co-Director

*Mission Statement:* We, at Nazareth Center, commit ourselves to live out our Incarnational Mission by being witnesses to God's unconditional love for all those who come to our Center.

Nazareth Center, situated on Newport's famous Cliff Walk, has a magnificent ocean view. It was opened by the Sisters of St. Chretienne as a retreat center so that their home and its prayerful setting could be enjoyed with you. The Center is for persons who need Quiet time to Pray, Reflect and Relax in a peace-filled atmosphere.

The Center offers a variety of programs and retreats. Its facilities also can be rented by non-profit organizations, such as Church, Educational and Professional groups. The house can accommodate up to 20 people by day and 10 overnight.

The Staff is available for Days, Evenings or Weekends of Prayer in parishes, communities or private homes. For further information please contact the Center.

Directed and Private Retreats are available at any time upon request. Fees:

| | |
|---|---|
| Directed | $35/day |
| | $160/5 days |
| | $220/7 days |
| Private | $30/day |
| Spiritual Direction | $20. |

To reserve your place, a non-refundable, non-transferable deposit is required: $30/weekend, $50/week. Balance due on arrival. Make reservations for programs and workshops 10 days in advance. Financial arrangements are negotiable if the fee is a burden. Call for information, including the current calendar of programs.

All weekend programs or retreats begin at 8PM on Friday and end Saturday after dinner. Guests have the option to stay overnight on Saturday by arrangement.

*Nazareth Center, Continued*

The Center is closed during the months of July and August. The pool is open in June and September. Smoking outdoors only.

Wishing to promote a wholistic approach to spirituality, Nazareth Center has made arrangements with a licensed massage therapist to offer massages to visitors at the Center.

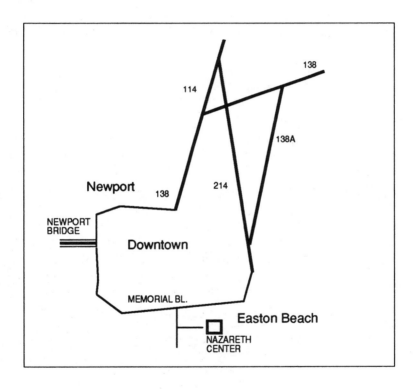

MEPKIN ABBEY
Cistercian Trappist Monastery
HC 69 Box 800
Moncks Corner SC 29461
☎ 803 761 8509
FAX 803 761 6719
Contact: The Guest Master

Men, women, and small groups of all denominations are received for weekends or week-long private retreats. There are accommodations for up to 8 guests: 4 private rooms with full baths, and a house which sleeps 4 (priority given to groups and married couples). Vegetarian meals, taken with the monastic community. Church services are open to all.

Large groups of up to 40 people are received for day visits. Conference room facilities are available. Make reservations with the Guest Master by mail, phone or fax. No charge, free-will offering accepted.

Located on the Cooper River, Mepkin was a rice plantation from the 1700s until 1911. In 1949, its last owners, Henry R. and Clare Boothe Luce, donated 3200 acres to the Cistercian Trappist monks from the Abbey of Gethsemani in Kentucky. Egg-farming is now the monastery industry.

Monks can arrange to meet you at the Charleston Airport Terminal, Amtrack Train Station or Greyhound Bus Station. There is also a Greyhound Station at Moncks Corner.

"Come to me...

listen and your
soul will live"

SPRINGBANK RETREAT CENTER
Route 2, Box 180
Kingstree SC 29556
☎ 803 382 3426 *General Information*
  803 382 9777 *Sabbatical Program*
  803 382 9778 *Individual & Weekend Retreats*

Springbank provides Guided, Private and Directed Retreats, 60-day Sabbaticals, Wellness Seminars, Depth Psychology, Creation-Centered Spirituality, Native American Spirituality, Workshops in the Healing Arts (music, massage, color, fiber, clay).

The Staff feel in harmony with a wholistic approach to life, centered in the Word, conscious of the importance of spiritual, mental and physical health, and the extraordinary power of creative energy. They hold a deep respect for all reality, and accept the responsibility to care for the Earth and to foster freedom and well-being in themselves and others.

Springbank is a place of hospitality and healing, located in a quiet, rural setting of South Carolina, on 58 wooded acres—live oak and magnolia trees, good biking and walking areas, simple, casual lifestyle.

Large conference/chapel area, air-conditioning, comfortable meeting rooms with fireplaces, overnight accommodations for 25 in mostly private rooms, art studio. Health conscious food.

Rates:
Weekend Retreat: $90, non-refundable $25 deposit when registering.
Private Retreat: $40 per day, overnight and meals.
Counselling and Spiritual Direction: $25 per session.
Healing Massage: $40
60-day Sabbatical: $2700
Airport transport: $25 per trip, (Florence or Charleston airports)
Bus or train terminals: $10 per trip.

Springbank is located 20 miles north of Kingstree, off Highway 527 on County Road S45-114.

**MOTHER OF GOD MONASTERY**
120 28th Avenue S.E.
Watertown SD 57201
☎ 605 886 6777
Contact: Ramona Fallon OSB

*Benedictine Sisters*

Call or write for information about retreats.

PENUEL RIDGE RETREAT CENTER
1440 Sams Creek Road
State Route 249
Ashland City  TN 37015
☎ 615 792 3734
Contact: Retreat Coordinator

Penuel Ridge Retreat is an Ecumenical Center founded in 1983 by a group of people identifying with the Judeo-Christian tradition of openness, compassion and liberation. People of all faiths and traditions are welcome.

'Penuel' comes from the Genesis story of Jacob who was transformed when he 'saw God face to face' at a place called Penuel. There are times when we, like Jacob, need time apart to meet God in a new way.

Penuel Ridge offers a quiet, hospitable setting to all who seek time and space to relax, to be out of doors, to pray or seek guidance or clarity for their life journey. Sit by the lake, journal, walk trails, or simply *be* in the presence of God.

*Individual Retreat:* for a day, overnight, or a longer period.

*Small Groups:* use facilities for their own retreats, supplying their own leadership, or requesting that Penuel Ridge provide a leader.

*Clearness Days:* for individuals or groups, for the purpose of seeking more clarity about life directions or career choices.

*Penuel Ridge Group Retreats:* on weekends throughout the year, announced in advance in retreat flyers. Retreats vary in length, include time for reflection alone, as well as time for discussion and sharing with others. Schedule mailed on request.

*Quiet Days:* once a month on a weekday, for anyone who wants space for reflection and rest. No schedule except for an optional opening meditation and closing reflection time.

*Rest Days:* for religious workers, scheduled one day each quarter, these 'Sabbath Rest Days' are especially for priests, rabbis, ministers and other religious workers who have responsibilities on weekends. The day begins with a presentation and the remainder of the day is for quiet, personal reflection.

*Spiritual Direction:* available on advance request.

*Penuel Ridge Retreat Center, Continued*

Call or write for fee schedule, and information on scholarships.

Accommodation: Attached to the main house are 2 bedrooms, bath, kitchenette and a meeting room.

The Howard Thurman House, a hermitage in the woods, has electric heat and lights, small refrigerator, microwave and chemical toilet.

The Dorothy Day House is equipped as the Thurman House, and is especially for those who are in the helping vocations, and for the troubled persons with whom they work. It may be used by others when available.

There is a small shelter by the lake for relaxation, picnics or camping for 1 or 2 people.

Meals are provided only for those programs sponsored by Penuel Ridge. Retreats sponsored by other groups are self-catered. Individual retreatants bring their own food.

Penuel Ridge is located on 120 acres, 20 miles west of Nashville, adjoining the Cheatham Wildlife Preserve. Trails wind through wooded ridges and around a tranquil, spring-fed lake.

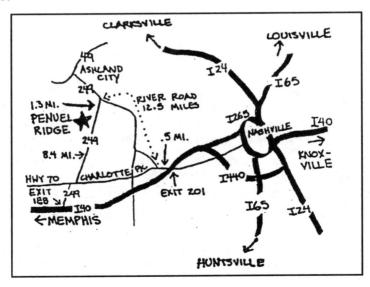

CHRISTIAN RENEWAL CENTER
1515 Hughes Road
Dickinson TX 77539
☎ 713 337 1312
Contact: Laverne Dawson

The Christian Renewal Center is staffed by the Missionary Oblates of Mary Immaculate, in Texas since 1849.

Facilities include 58 single rooms, cabins, bayou, swimming pool. Located on 52 wooded acres. Meals provided. Daily Eucharist, the Sacrament of Reconciliation, and Spiritual Direction is available.

Donation requested: $35 per day.

**MOUNT CARMEL CENTER**
4600 West Davis
Dallas TX 75211
☎ 214 331 6224
Contact: Father Director

Mount Carmel Center is a contemplative center operated by the Discalced Carmelite Fathers of the Southwest Province since 1974.

In the context of a praying community, Mount Carmel provides a contemplative approach to the apostolate for which St. Teresa of Avila and St. John of the Cross founded their Carmelite Friars, four centuries ago—the promulgation of the interior life. Through its programs, Mount Carmel Center seeks to foster among the Christian community the contemplative dimension—an openness to transcendence, a disposition to commune with the infinite mystery of God. Hence it has been called a house of spiritual direction.

The programs at the Center are primarily of two kinds. First, lecture series on different aspects of Christian spirituality are presented regularly during Advent and Lent. The goal of the Center is to provide a platform for all the serious traditions of Christian asceticism and mysticism, in dialogue with non-Christian traditions.

Second, Mount Carmel provides residential facilities for small-group contemplative retreats, and opens its facilities for non-residential days of prayer to groups which provide their own director.

Ideally, a group retreat here will be for persons of the same sex (because of limited restroom facilities). There is one prepared meal a day on most weekdays at noon. Rarely on Sundays. It is difficult to provide space for private retreats on weekends because of the programs going on, but private retreatants usually can be accommodated on weekdays.

The *House of Silence* offers simple, rustic accommodations. Summer Study-Retreats include classes, private counselling, a contemplative celebration of the Eucharist, and participation in the Liturgy of the Hours. There is plenty of time and space for solitude and private prayer. A small Byzantine Oratory, and a larger contemporary chapel are always available, and the wooded grounds are spacious and inviting.

*Mount Carmel Center, Continued*

Throughout the year, Mount Carmel also offers special programs and liturgical celebrations connected with the major seasons and feasts of the Church and the Carmelite Order. These include solemn celebrations of the Eucharist, directed meditations, lectures, and the opportunity to share in the Divine Office. The Community Liturgy is open to the public throughout the year.

Mount Carmel Center is first and foremost a monastery of Discalced Carmelite Friars, a community dedicated to a life of contemporary austerity and the search for God through contemplation and the service of Christ's Church.

For retreatants, the community offers a structure and a support system. The extent of the individual's involvement with the prayer schedule of the community varies with the needs and wishes of the retreatant.

Visitors coming to services should call to verify the schedule.

Write or call the Center for information on upcoming events, and to schedule a retreat.

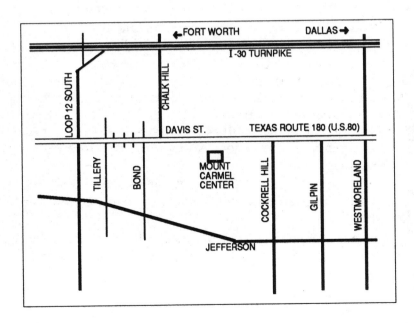

CORPUS CHRISTI ABBEY
HCR 2,  Box 6300
Sandia  TX 78383
☎  512 547 3257
FAX 512 547 5184
Contact: Director

A small Benedictine monastic community. This retreat center is situated on 110 acres of lakeshore property.

Facilities include monastic chapel, abbey library, monastery and retreat center, dining rooms, and 35 simple but complete bedrooms. Rooms are private and semi-private, air-conditioned, all with linens and private bath.

A Retreat Center staff member is in charge of the complex at all times, and will take care of special requests.

A spirit of silence prevails in the residence buildings out of respect for people who wish to sleep, read or pray.

Individual monks and staff members are available for spiritual direction, counselling, and Sacramental Reconciliation. Retreatants are invited and welcome to pray the Liturgy of the Hours and the Eucharist with the monastic community.

Casual dress is the norm—no shorts in church.

The monks of Corpus Christi Abbey want the Center to be open to all. Retreatants are asked to enclose whatever donation they can in envelopes provided in the rooms. The expenses of the Abbey for weekend retreats are $60 per person, $90 per married couple. Private Retreat: $20 per day; Directed Retreat: $25 per day. Group rates will be negotiated with each particular retreat group or organization. A deposit is required for group reservations.

Call or write for calendar of events, general information such as prayer times, retreat center guidelines, maps and history of the Abbey.

The Abbey is located approximately 50 miles from Corpus Christi, Texas, travel time from downtown—about 1 hour.

WESTON PRIORY
Benedictine Monks
58 Priory Hill Road
Weston VT 05161
Contact: Guest Brother.


Weston Priory was founded in 1953 by the late Abbot Leo Rudloff of Dormition Abbey, Jerusalem, Israel.

Guests usually stay 3 days to 1 week. Make reservations at least 4 months in advance—booked for individual and group retreats months ahead.

*Priory Guest House* —5 to 6 men guests take meals with the brothers.

*Morningside* —5 women guests, weekdays. Accommodation varies according to the time of year. Meals are taken with the brothers, a 5-minute walk to the Priory.

*Group Retreats* —no formal, directed retreats. Bring your own food and prepare meals in the Guest House. 3 Guest Houses accommodate 3 to 8 adults.

Donations are accepted.

Located 4 miles north of Weston, VT, on the edge of the Green Mountain National Forest.

SAINT ANNE'S SHRINE
Edmundite Fathers and Brothers
Isle Lamotte  VT 05463
☎ 802 928 3362   (Office open year-round)
Contact: Director

Many praying faithful lay before St. Anne both their spiritual and physical tribulations, knowing that in this popular saint, devotion to whom extends back to the first centuries of the Church, they have an interested and powerful intercessor.

The Fathers of St. Edmund, who have staffed the Shrine since 1904, are able to accommodate large numbers of people with ease. The Shrine offers a full range of devotional activities, culminating in the Solemn Triduum of St. Anne on July 23, 24 & 25, marking her Feast Day on July 26.

Thousands of pilgrims visit the Shrine each season to participate in the Eucharistic Celebrations that are held in the open-air pavilion which affords a closeness to nature.

The majestic granite statue of Samuel de Champlain is located on the Shrine grounds on the site where it is claimed he landed in 1609. It was sculpted for Expo '67. The Shrine is also the home of the magnificent gold-leafed statue of Our Lady of Lourdes which once stood atop the Cathedral of Burlington.

Also on the grounds are a souvenir shop, rustic grottoes, and The Way of the Cross, nestled among tall pines on the shores of Lake Champlain.

A cafeteria serving pilgrims and visitors is open daily, and there are plenty of picnic facilities for families and groups who come to spend a day in prayer and peace. There is also a beautiful sandy beach which may be used for swimming, and a large dock for tourists and pilgrims who wish to visit the Shrine by boat.

The Shrine is open daily from mid-May to mid-October.

# MONASTERY OF THE IMMACULATE HEART OF MARY
HCR #13, Box 11
Westfield VT 05874
☎ 802 744 6525
Contact: Guestmistress

The Monastery of the Immaculate Heart of Mary was founded in 1981 by the Abbaye Sainte-Marie des Deux Montagnes, Canada. The 11th century Abbey of Sainte Pierre of Solesmes, France, is the origin and center of the Congregation. It has 20 monasteries of monks and 8 of nuns in 9 countries of Europe, Africa, North America and Central America.

At Westfield, there is a small guest house with 3 rooms for ladies, outside the enclosure, but inside the monastery. Private Retreats. Rate: $25 per day.

Mass is at 10AM—Gregorian Chant and the Latin Liturgy of Vatican II.

NAZARETH HOUSE OF PRAYER
Route 2, Box 277
Gate City VA 24251
☎ 703 386 7428
Contact: Staff: Sr. Corinne Myers RSM, Director
Sr. Catherine Laboure BUSAM, OSF
Sr. Carolyn Brink RSM

Simplicity and a peaceful, homelike environment characterize the Nazareth House of Prayer, set in the natural beauty of the Clinch Mountains in Appalachia.

There is accommodation for 9 people in 7 private rooms. Healthy, homecooked meals.

| | |
|---|---|
| Directed and Special Retreats: | $35 per day |
| Private Retreat | $25 per day |
| Weekend Retreat | $45 |
| Guided Weekend Experience | $65 |
| Solitude Experience in Hermitage | $15 (provide own food) |
| | $25 (meals provided) |
| Spiritual Direction | $15 per hour |

Nazareth House is 6 miles to the east of Gate City on Route 71. It is accessible by car, bus and plane. Tri-Cities Airport, serving Bristol, Kingsport and Johnson City TN, is 50 minutes away. The Greyhound bus comes in to Kingsport TN, 30 minutes away. Transportation can be provided from these places, and a donation is expected.

**TRINITY HOUSE**
638 Flynn Drive
Front Royal VA 22630
☎ 703 635 1495 *or* 703 636 9990
Contact: The Director

Trinity House offers traditional Vocation Retreats for young Catholic women seeking God's holy will in their lives. Retreatants are invited to stay from 1 to 5 days in a quiet, simple monastic setting in the Virginia Mountains. Spiritual Direction is available. A reference is required from a priest, sister, or other person in ministry work.

Women may also come for 1 or 2 days of reflection in Private Retreat, and then do some sight-seeing. Women who are in the area on church-related business, or who are seeking employment in the area, are invited to stay a few nights.

Trinity House was once 3 separate cabins, and has 3 beds in the comfortably furnished guest room, with private bath. The Chapel is close-by.

Every guest, visitor or retreatant has the opportunity to pray with Sr. Gemma, a Visitation nun. Though silence is observed for most of the retreat, especially during meals and reflection time, Sister always makes herself available for consultation.

Spiritual books and tapes are available for use by retreatants, and they are welcome to walk around the wooded grounds. For Mass, retreatants have to go off the mountain to St. John Church of Christendom, 20 minutes away.

Call or write for further information about this House of Prayer and Discernment.

THE WELL RETREAT CENTER
18047 Quiet Way
Smithfield VA 23430
☎ 804 255 2366
Contact: Diane Weymouth or Sr. Nancy Healy SFCC, Co-Directors

The Well is a small Retreat Center, for both Group and Private Retreats. Accommodations include 32 beds in 16 rooms. Rate: $30 overnight.

**POOR CLARE MONASTERY**
28 Harpersville Road
Newport News VA 23601
Contact: Mother Mary Colette PCC

The Chapel is available to visitors seeking a place for quiet prayer and reflection.

The public is invited to celebrate daily Mass with the nuns in their chapel at 7AM, and holy hour on Sundays, with Vespers, Rosary and Benediction of the Blessed Sacrament.

Each year from August 2-11 there is a public novena in honor of St. Clare at 7:15PM.

## MONASTERY OF OUR LADY OF THE ANGELS
Route 2, Box 288-A
Crozet VA 22932
Contact: The Guestsister

This Monastery offers Group and Private Retreats in a prayerful, quiet, reflective atmosphere, close to nature and God. Conferences and Spiritual Direction are not provided, however; a schedule of prayer times at the monastery is posted, and guests are most welcome to join the sisters in worship from the guests' section of the Chapel. The Sisters' section of the monastery and the cheesemaking buildings are not open to the public or retreatants.

Facilities include 2 log cabins, the larger built in 1810 and completely modernized, 2 full baths, shared kitchen. 2 people can share this cabin and maintain privacy. There are 2 double beds, 3 singles, a pull-out couch and a sleep-chair in the living room, and space in the loft for sleeping bags.

The smaller cabin, a pre-fabricated model from the 1950s, has 2 bedrooms, a kitchen/dining area, 1 bath and 2 single beds.

Linens and towels are supplied for single guests, groups of more than 3 are asked to bring their own. Any particular group may visit one time per year.

Both cabins are stocked with canned goods, orange juice, bread and other staples. Milk and other fresh food must be brought by the retreatant.

The cabins are situated beside a pond near Pigeon Top Mountain, a mile from the monastery by the road. A car is necessary. No pets. Arrive before 5PM and pick up your cabin key at the front door of the monastery.

Write in advance to make reservations, giving the preferred date and two alternates. A non-refundable deposit of $20 confirms your reservation. There is no fixed fee, but a donation is appreciated. Please inform the Guestsister as soon as possible, if cancelling.

Because of heavy demand, the length of stay for an individual is limited to about one week. A nine-day retreat Friday to the second Sunday, is possible. For a weekend retreat, arrive on Friday and leave by 3PM Sunday.

## ST. MARTIN'S ABBEY GUESTHOUSE
5300 Pacific Avenue S.E.
Lacey WA 98503
☎ 206 438 4457 *or* 206 491 4700
Contact: Guestmaster

St. Martin's is provided in the spirit of Benedictine hospitality, for personal retreats, a quiet time for spiritual reflection at the guesthouse and around the college campus.

All are invited to join the monks in daily worship, at Mass and the Divine Prayer Hours.

The guesthouse can accommodate 16 people in twin-bedded rooms, each with desk, clothes-rack and sink. The rooms are tastefully decorated. Showers are in the bathrooms halfway down the hall. There is a parlor for quiet conversation, coffee and tea. Spiritual reading material is available.

In the hallway of the guesthouse is a cabinet of articles for sale, made by the monks of St. Martin's Abbey.

Call or write for further information and to make reservations in advance.

*Let all guests who arrive be received like Christ, for He is going to say, 'I came as a guest, and you received me.'*

–Rule of St. Benedict, Chapter 53

Saint
Benedict

## HOLDEN VILLAGE
Chelan
Washington 98816
Contact: Registrar

Holden Village is a Lutheran Retreat Center. Stays of one or more nights are possible. The night before may be spent in the B&B ($33 for 2 people), then take the ferry early in the morning for Holden Village. One may join structured activities if desired.

Cost: $46 per person for the first night; $215 for 7 nights. The first night's fee is the deposit, which is returnable if cancellation is made four weeks prior to arrival date.

There is no phone at the Center, but there is an answering service at Field's Point and messages usually reach the Village within 24 hours. A nurse is usually on duty in case of emergency.

This historic copper-mining town is surrounded by a glacier peak system.

Write for further information and to make reservations.

KAIROS HOUSE OF PRAYER
West 1714 Stearns Road
Spokane WA 99208
☎ 509 466 2187
Contact: Guest Sister

Kairos House of Prayer is a sanctuary for those seeking peace and quiet, at the end of a private lane on 27 acres of wooded hilltop, 2300 feet above sea-level. There is a large house, a barn and 7 hermitages nestled among Ponderosa pines and glacier rocks.

This contemplative community has established a rhythm of prayer, work and study. It assembles for meditation at 8AM, 11:30AM and 5PM. Celebration of the Eucharist is contingent on the availability of a priest.

Retreats can take place here from a day to several weeks or months. Individuals can stay in very comfortable and private hermitages overlooking the valley. The wind sighs through the pines and the night sky is dazzling. Vegetarian meals are served in the kitchen-dining room of the main house.

Accommodations include 9 private rooms in the main house and renovated barn, and 7 hermitages with electricity, porta-potty (or short walk to shared baths), hot-plate, frig and bottled water. Meals are taken with the community and are eaten in silence.

Kairos offers Centering Meditation, and work on deep relaxation and concentration, breathing methods, and physical postures. There are country roads for walking.

Open year-round. Cost: $28.50 per day.

Call or write for further information and reservations.

## LOMA CENTER FOR RENEWAL
Lutheran Outdoor Ministries in Western Washington
3607 228th Avenue S.E.
Issaquah WA 98027
☎ 206 392 1871 *or in W. Washington:* 800 464 5662
Contact: Guest Services Coordinator

The LOMA Center is primarily a retreat and conference center for small and large groups.

Personal Retreats are limited to 3 nights and 4 days. Each reservation accommodates up to 3 people. Call at least 24 hours in advance. Donations are accepted, but there is no charge for making a personal retreat.

A private room is guaranteed, linens provided. Each room has a desk dresser overlooking nature, a sink with cup and soap, full closet, bedstand, reading light, single, twin, or double bed. Some rooms are carpeted. Specify your preference. Baths down the hall.

If the center is serving a guest group, personal retreatants are guaranteed one of their popular meals each meal-time. A table is set aside in the dining room, and personal retreatants are welcome at the staff table. When meals are not served, individuals can use the microwave and frig in the dining room. There is an open beverage bar with tea, juice, cocoa, etc.

Prayer time each Tuesday and Thursday morning in the Chapel: all are welcome to join the staff for a reflection to begin the day.

The outdoor hot tub is well maintained and ready for use. Swimming in the nearby heated indoor pool. A library, nature trails, bicycling, horseshoes and volleyball are available.

Some LOMA staff live at the Center, and provide hospitality as Christ calls us to do. They believe that each of us is to care for one another and ourselves.

THE PRIORY SPIRITUALITY CENTER
500 College Street N.E.
Lacey  WA 98516
☎   206 438 2595  *Center*
     206 438 1771  *Priory*
FAX 206 438 9236
Contact: Hospitality Coordinator

The Priory Spirituality Center is a house of prayer, a Christ-Centered holy space for those who seek God. It is an expression of St. Placid Community's commitment to peace and hospitality.

We welcome individuals and groups of all faiths: those seeking a closer relationship with God and desiring time and space for inner renewal, spiritual studies, faith experiences, or personal reflection in an atmosphere of creative quiet.

Private Retreats can be for a few hours, a day or overnight, with or without Spiritual Direction. The Center provides for Group Retreats and programs. A brochure with a schedule of programs and directions to the Center is available on request.

We also provide Outreach Programs. Guests can participate in the monastic experience, and are invited to join the Sisters in the Liturgy of the Hours and other worship services.

There are overnight facilities for 10 retreatants, 19 if rooms are shared. There is a Chapel, a small prayer room, library, 4 multi-purpose rooms and wooded trails.

The Priory is easy to find: exit 109 off Interstate 5.

GOOD COUNSEL FRIARY
Route 7, Box 183 (Tyrone Road)
Morgantown  WV 26505
☎   304 594 1714
FAX 304 594 9247

Good Counsel Friary offers Group and Private Retreats. Also, Christian visitors are welcome. In summer, retreatants may also work with the poor.

Modest accommodations. Donation.

# SINSINAWA MOUND CENTER
Sinsinawa WI 53824
☎ 608 748 4411
FAX 608 748 4491
Contact: Retreat Office

Sinsinawa Mound Center is an ecumenical retreat and conference Center located in Southwest Wisconsin. Sponsored by the Sinsinawa Dominican Sisters, the 450 acre site contains the Center, Dominican Motherhouse, farmland and woodlands. Visitors can experience the beauty of the Mississippi Valley.

Facilities include: Queen of the Rosary Chapel, a bookshop, library, meeting rooms and lounges. The Alcove, for private retreatants desiring quiet space, offers comfortable private sitting rooms, a kitchenette and reflection resources.

The kitchen serves buffet-style meals with delicious homemade breads.

The following Retreat Spirituality Services are available: Spiritual Guidance, Private Directed Retreat, Private Retreat, Sinsinawa Staff Led Retreat, Days of Prayer, Off-Site Retreat. —For further information on these services, contact Marie Louise Seckar OP, at 748 4411. A current program booklet with information regarding costs and directions, will be sent on request.

Sinsinawa Mound is part of the area in Southwestern Wisconsin referred to by Native Americans as 'Manitoumie,' translated as: 'Where the Spirit dwells.' Those who live here, work here and visit, recognize that Manitoumie still describes this holy place, and they are part of the 'Spirit' of Sinsinawa Mound. In the Dominican tradition of hospitality, you are invited to visit the Mound.

*Mission Statement:*

We, the Retreat Spirituality Department of the Sinsinawa Mound Center, seek to provide ecumenical opportunities for deepening and re-creating our relationships to Self, One Another, Earth and God through prayer, study, and the experience of being 'in the land where the Spirit dwells.'

183

HOLY HILL
National Shrine of Mary Help of Christians
Discalced Carmelite Friars
1525 Carmel Road
Hubertus WI 53033
☎ 414 628 1838

This is a House of Prayer for all people, in a setting of natural beauty. Visible for miles from all directions, the spires of Holy Hill seem to soar into the heavens, The Neo-Romanesque church with priceless stained-glass windows and magnificent mosaics, has a breathtaking view of the southern Kettle Moraine countryside.

There are two guest houses for overnight visitors and retreat groups, combined capacity: 57. There are shared baths in the Olde Monastery Inn Guest House and private baths in the new guest house. There are no Private Directed Retreats, but Self-Directed Retreats are encouraged. Guest rooms and group retreat facilities are simple but comfortable.

Meals are provided for Group Retreats only. The guest house kitchen is available to private retreatants for meal preparation. The Olde Monastery Inn cafeteria produces nourishing and tasty meals and simple snacks, and a Sunday brunch, and is open weekends and daily from June 1st to October 31st.

Cost: single occupancy—$26 per night; double occupancy—$40 per night.

For a Day of Recollection, a group may reserve a conference room and use a private chapel in the Olde Monastery Inn Guest House at a cost of $75. Both conference room and chapel accommodate 45 people. Advance reservations are necessary.

Holy Hill is on the National and State Registers of Historic Places. There is free admission and parking. A good-will offering is appreciated.

One may visit the Shrine Chapel, gift store, gourmet bake shop, or enjoy time spent at the picnic grounds. Church and restrooms are handicapped- accessible. For a quiet day, plan to visit during the week. A booklet, *Pilgrim Walk,* to aid in a self-guided tour of the Shrine, can be purchased at the gift shop.

*Holy Hill, Continued*

Pilgrims may walk along the one-half mile outdoor Way of the Cross with its 14 groups of life-size sculptures. Others may pray at the Lourdes Grotto or stroll around 400 wooded acres, crossed by Wisconsin's Ice Age Trail. In Summer and Fall one may climb 178 steps to the top observation tower inside one of the church spires for a glimpse of rural surroundings and the skyline of Milwaukee on the horizon.

Special events at Holy Hill include: Live Nativity; Religious Concerts; Arts and Crafts Fair; a full range of Religious Services and Devotions. Send for a schedule of Masses and Devotions and other information on the Shrine and facilities.

All groups of over 15 people are asked to notify the monastery office with the date they plan to visit, and a detailed itinerary will be sent to the group leader. Call in advance to make arrangements for one of the staff to give a Shrine Presentation with a brief history of Holy Hill and the Carmelite Order. This 25-minute presentation is available only when pre-scheduled.

Holy Hill is located 30 miles north of Milwaukee, 70 miles east of Madison, and 110 miles north of Chicago.

THE DE KOVEN CENTER
600 21st Street
Racine WI 53403
☎ 414 633 6401
Contact: Conference and Retreat Coordinator

The English Gothic-style buildings of the DeKoven Center originally housed Racine College, an Episcopal preparatory school for boys, founded in 1852. Soon after the school's closing in 1933, St. Mary's Home in Chicago and the Community of St. Mary assumed management of the property.

Following the tradition of prayer and learning established by the Rev. Dr. James DeKoven during his long tenure as headmaster of Racine College, the Sisters offered summer camps, retreats and conferences in these historic buildings until 1986, when ownership was transferred to the Episcopal Diocese of Milwaukee.

The campus continues to host a variety of activities, including retreats and conferences in Taylor Hall, sporting events in the gymnasium and pool, weddings and church gatherings in St. John's Chapel, a Montessori school and an arts school in the East Building, and receptions and seminars in the Great Hall.

The buildings are listed in the National Register of Historic Places. Taylor Hall, built in 1867, provides accommodation and meeting space for a variety of adult groups.

Besides welcoming groups that seek a place of meeting, the Center sponsors a number of retreats and conferences throughout the year, open to all. These include Conducted Silent Retreats, Continuing Education Conferences and workshops focusing on current issues in the Church. All DeKoven conferences are offered from a perspective of prayer, spirituality and theological reflection.

The Hermitage, a separate living space in Taylor Hall, is ideal for Private Retreats and Sabbaticals. 4 bedrooms, bath, dining room, kitchen, provide privacy and quiet for individuals for a day or for several days. Small groups wishing to prepare their meals together also use The Hermitage for retreats and meetings.

St. John's Chapel is set in the center of the campus, and was built in 1864. It is open to wedding guests, retreatants and various communities at prayer. It can accommodate up to 200. There is a fine pipe organ in the choir loft, a vaulted ceiling and beautiful Belgian stained-glass windows.

*DeKoven Center, Continued*

The Great Hall in the East Building, facing Lake Michigan, was built in 1871 as the Refectory for Racine College. It is used for many events from business seminars to wedding receptions and madrigal dinners. Kitchen and restrooms and seating for 200.

The Gymnasium is available year-round for league basketball, volleyball etc., as well as individual and group rental. Recent renovations have restored the 1913 Italian mosaic tile which lines the pool. 6-foot windows create a year-round pleasant atmosphere. In addition to DeKoven sponsored activities, the pool is available on an hourly basis for individual and group rental.

The Gardens and grounds of the 34 acre campus contain a variety of trees, flora and fauna. Picnic tables are available for private reading or family gatherings. There are walkways among the trees and along the lakeshore. The Bishop's Garden is a favorite spot for quiet meditation and study.

The Center is halfway between Chicago and Milwaukee. Racine is about 1 hour north of O'Hare Airport, and 30 minutes south of Milwaukee's Mitchell Airport. Bus, train and taxi services are readily available to Racine, and to the nearby town of Sturtevant.

Call or write for current rates and a schedule of events.

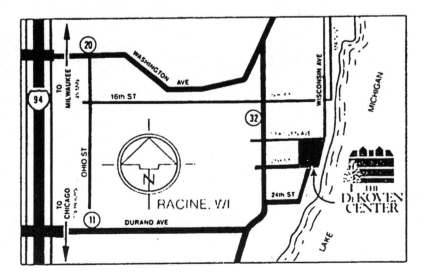

THE CONVENT HOUSE
Route 1, Box 161
Cashton WI 54619
☎ 608 823 7992  *or*  608 823 7906
Contact: Guestsister

The Convent House is the residence of the Franciscan Sisters since the 19th century. Newly redecorated, this spacious house offers a peaceful sleep and a tasty breakfast. 4 rooms are available with shared bath. A deposit is required to hold your reservation. Pets and smoking outside only. Indoor bike security. The Convent House is operated as a B & B during the busy summer season.

People may make a Private Retreat during the off-season, November–May. The room rate is discounted if you do your own cooking. The pastor at the parish church is available for Confession, Mass and Spiritual Direction if requested.

We are situated on St. Mary's Ridge, alongside the historic St. Mary's Ridge Church (erected in 1856), and the official U.S. Department of Agriculture Midwest farm-scene which is displayed in Washington DC and in the Corn Palace at Mitchell, SD.

We offer country hospitality and relaxation with local folks. The Convent House is close to canoeing on the Kickapoo River, biking the Elroy-Sparta Trail, hiking in Wild Cat Mountain State Park, horseback riding, skiing, tour a dairy farm, etc.

The area also has a large Amish community where furniture, quilts, baked goods and many other handcrafted items may be purchased.

Call or write for current rates or to make your reservation.

CONVENT OF THE HOLY NATIVITY
101 East Division Street
Fond du Lac  WI 54935
Contact: Guestsister

The Convent of the Holy Nativity offers Private Retreats lasting a few days. A free will offering is suggested. Write in advance for further information and to make a reservation.

## MARYNOOK RETREAT AND CONFERENCE CENTER
500 South 12th Street
P.O. Box 9
Galesville WI 54630
☎ 608 582 2789 or 608 526 9550
Contact: Administrative Assistant

Marynook is a Jesus Christ centered ecumenical retreat and conference center which provides a haven of prayer and opportunity for spiritual growth.

*Private Retreats:* Personal and self-directed retreats of varying lengths can be arranged at any time. Suggested donation: $40 per day. Long term retreats vary in cost.

*Personal Directed Retreats:* Available throughout the year, of varying length, as arranged with the Director of the Center. Daily meeting with a staff person. Suggested donation: $45 per day.

*Youth Retreats:* Churches are encouraged to bring their young people to Marynook as part of their spiritual formation programs.

*Parish Council Retreats:* Marynook offers a retreat especially designed for parish councils, offering time to share vision and to learn the art of communal discernment. An excellent opportunity for all churches.

Facilities include 40 comfortable sleeping rooms accommodating 80 people, bedding and towels provided. There is a large conference room and dining room for meetings. Each dormitory has a lounge for quiet conversation or small group interaction. The Eucharistic Chapel is a good place for private or community prayer. There is an excellent retreat library in St. Joseph's, and a gift shop open to the public—books on prayer, art pieces, cards, etc.

Marynook is surrounded by 40 acres of park-like grounds, a swimming pool, gym and volleyball court. It is located 20 minutes north of LaCrosse, 15 miles south of Winona MN, 2.5 hours south of Minneapolis, and 2.5 hours west of Madison. State Highways 35 and 53 pass within a few miles of the Center.

The Center operates on the gifts and offerings of those who use it. Retreats are offered to all who desire to come. Those who can, give out of their abundance, and those who cannot, give from what they have.

The prayer community invites all to join in praying the Divine Office as well as in Adoration of the Blessed Sacrament, Bible studies and discussions.

As you enter these beautiful grounds along the pine-columned road, you will be greeted by a stately white building, built in 1862. This landmark is where the second university of the State of Wisconsin was founded: Galesville University. It has a long and very interesting history of service to God's people within the Christian tradition.

Since 1984, Marynook has served as a privately-owned ecumenical retreat center, originally under the auspices of the Society of Mary. It is run on the faith of the volunteers and members of Marynook Inc., who have kept the dream alive.

The apostles said to the Lord, 'Increase our faith.' The Lord replied, 'Were your faith the size of a mustard seed, you could say to this mulberry tree, *be uprooted and planted in the sea,* and it would obey you.' Luke 17:6

RIDGEWOOD RETREAT CENTER
Route 1, Box 3150
County YY
Neshkoro  WI 54960
☎  414 293 4488
FAX 414 293 4361
Contact: Director

Ridgewood is a 48-bed retreat center offering Group Retreats and Personal and Semi-Personal Retreats. Costs: overnight, $15 per person, excluding meals.

Meal service is available if the group size warrants it. A variety of meal service options from family-style to buffet, and snack service are offered according to your group's need. The aroma of freshly-brewed hazel-nut coffee and a basket of crisp orchard apples awaits you. There are several restaurants nearby.

Facilities include comfortable meeting areas for groups of 5 to 50. Each location has a cozy fireplace. The Lucerne library is next to the larger meeting area. Full bed and towel linen service is provided. Audio-visual equipment and copying facilities (for a small fee) are provided. Off-site tours to local attractions can be arranged.

In warm weather, there is canoeing, sailing, swimming, tennis, etc; and cross-country skiing and ice-skating in winter. Nearby Nordic Mountain offers full-service downhill skiing.

Ridgewood Retreat Center is owned and operated by the Wisconsin Conference of the United Methodist Church. It enjoys a five-decade heritage of providing retreats and conferences, camping and recreational opportunities.

The Center is located off State Route 73 on County Road YY, 5 miles south of Wautoma, Wisconsin.

# HOLY NAME RETREAT HOUSE
Chambers Island
Wisconsin
*Inquiries to:*
Holy Name Retreat House
P.O. Box 23825
Green Bay WI 54305
☎ 414 437 7531 (Green Bay) *or* 414 734 1112 (Fox Valley)
Contact: Administrators

With its unique location on Chambers Island, and the beautiful surroundings, Holy Name Retreat House offers a place to get away to relax, pray, listen and reflect. Here is the opportunity to be alone, to cleanse the mind, to heal the soul, to communicate with oneself and God.

The retreat experience contains many elements: Mass, group prayer, presentations by a priest, sister or lay person, personal counseling, silence, private reading, good meals, sleep and the scenic beauty of the island. There are comfortable lounges, a library and a Chapel.

Retreats are offered for men and women, religious, couples, seminarians and people in recovery. There are different kinds of retreats of varying lengths: Silent, Healing, Private, Charismatic and Directed. Send for the current retreat schedule and rates. Holy Name is owned and operated by the Catholic Diocese of Green Bay. Non-Catholics are encouraged to participate in the retreat experience.

There are no stores or transportation on the island—mainly private cottages and the Retreat House. Bicycles are available for use on the trails. Canoes and fishing available at the inland lake. Take casual clothes, walking shoes and a light jacket are suggested.

The House is about 7 miles off the shore of Fish Creek in Door County, WI, and is accessible only by boat. Each retreat begins and ends with a 45-minute trip across Green Bay in the Retreat House boat, the *Quo Vadis*.

The Retreat House is primarily supported by the offering of retreatants, a contribution is requested. Advance registration and a non-refundable $20 registration fee is required. Inability to pay the entire retreat fee should not be a deterrent to making a retreat. Write for complete information.

RACINE DOMINICAN RETREAT CENTER
Siena Center
5635 Erie Street
Racine  WI 53402
☎ 414 639 4100
Contact: S. Grace Smith, Director of Arrangements

Call or write for complete information on retreats and activities.

## SAN BENITO MONASTERY
Benedictine Sisters
P.O. Box 520
Dayton WY 82836
☎ 307 655 9013
Contact: Guest Sister

San Benito Monastery is a community of Benedictine Sisters who live, pray, work and attempt to create an environment in which others may share in their prayer and way of life. Guests of all faiths who desire to spend time apart from their daily activities are welcome to come for a day, a weekend, or longer.

We offer Private, Guided or Directed Retreats. Books and tapes are available for use by retreatants. There are 6 private rooms for guests. Suggested offering: $25 per day. Casual clothing and walking shoes are recommended.

The Monastery is situated on 38 acres near the Big Horn Mountains. It is a 20 minute drive to the top of the mountains, and less than that to the beautiful Tongue River Canyon. It is a 5 hour drive to Yellowstone National Park. San Benito is a space for the appreciation of beauty, the presence of God, and a release from the stress of the demands of society.

Guests can be met at the Sheridan, Wyoming airport–a 40 minute drive from the Monastery. Write or call for reservations.

Our Lord moves among the pots and pans.

# HOUSES OF PRAYER
# & RETREAT CENTERS
# IN CANADA

MARIAN CENTRE
10528  98 Street
Edmonton,  Alberta  T5H 2N4
Contact: Any of the Staff

The Marian Centre is a field house of the Madonna House Apostolate.

This building in downtown Edmonton houses a soup kitchen for transient men. But there are also rooms set aside for 'poustinia' (a Russian word for 'desert'). One goes to a room for 24 hours with only the Bible, some bread, and tea or coffee or water, for a time of solitude, silence and prayer. One also has access to our chapel. While these rooms are in a wing separate from the soup kitchen, our daily life goes on as normal.

Contact the Marian Centre for more information about spending this short time apart from worldly cares.

**FCJ CHRISTIAN LIFE CENTRE**
219 19th Avenue S.W.
Calgary, Alberta T2S OC8
☎ 403 228 4215

The FCJ Christian Life Centre offers Private Retreats, Group Retreats and Days of Recollection.

The Centre can accommodate 48 people overnight: 15 in double rooms and 18 in single rooms. There are 2 dining rooms.

The Elbow River runs through the grounds, located 10 blocks from downtown Calgary.

Call or write for further information.

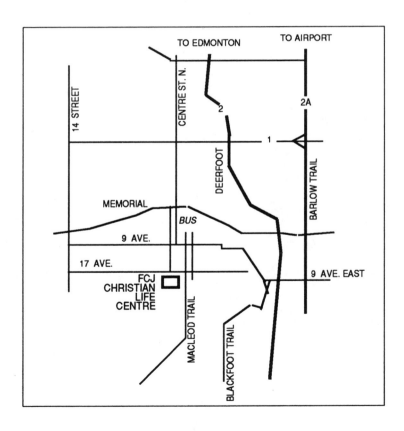

## VANCOUVER SCHOOL OF THEOLOGY
6000 Iona Drive
Vancouver, British Columbia V6T 1L4
☎ 604 228 9031
FAX 604 228 0189
Contact: Supervisor of Facilities Operations

Conference facilities and year-round retreat facilities are available. Individual guests are welcome. VST expects the activities of groups using its facilities to be in harmony with the aims and objectives of the School.

During the academic term from early September to the end of April, there are a few twin-bedded rooms with bathrooms down the hall available among the room and board residence. In summer, single rooms with baths down the hall—few available in July. During the summer a housing assistant is available from 8:30AM to 11PM—on call during the academic year. Linens are provided, laundry facilities. No smoking in public areas. University Hospital is a full-service facility available for visitors' needs. Vancouver School of Theology is located on the campus of the University of British Columbia (UBC) in West Side Vancouver.

Food Service is available on a cash basis during the academic year and when a group of over 50 uses the facilities during the summer. Call or write for a group information package describing the facilities, current rates, map and further information.

Several parking lots are available May–August. Parking is free with room rental. During the academic year, parking is limited, but the UBC Parkade is nearby. Bus service to downtown Vancouver.

One of the major Canadian theological libraries is open to anyone: over 80,000 items, with subscriptions to 350 periodicals on Biblical studies, Christianity, doctrinal and practical theology and Protestant (especially Canadian) denominations, with emphasis on VST's supporting denominations: The Anglican Church of Canada, The United Church of Canada and The Presbyterian Church in Canada.

Use of the Epiphany Chapel must be approved by VST's Principal. The Iona Chapel is available at all times for quiet prayer and meditation.

*Vancouver School of Theology, Continued*

VST has a fine view of the ocean and mountains, and is near several attractions on the UBC campus and surrounding area.

The Aquatic Centre, with both indoor and outdoor pool, weight room, sauna and whirlpool, is open most days.

The Museum of Anthropology holds a world-renowned collection of native artifacts, and houses an extensive collection of totem poles. It is usually free of charge on Tuesdays.

The Rose, Nitobe and Botanical Gardens are all available to visitors.

The UBC bookstore is one of the largest in Canada.

The Student Union Building contains restaurants, bars, a theatre, a bank, stores and the SUBWAY Cafeteria.

Pacific Spirit Park has lots of hiking trails and is a good example of the West Coast rainforest ecosystem. The entrance to the Park is a 10-minute walk away.

There is also a choice of beaches near the VST campus. A housing assistant can give directions to a suitable beach.

SAINT BENEDICT'S EDUCATIONAL CENTRE
225 Masters Avenue, RR 1B
Winnipeg, Manitoba R3C 4A3
Contact: Administrator

St. Benedict's Educational Center offers Retreats, Conferences and Meetings. Please write for complete details and a schedule of events.

NOVA NADA
Wilderness Retreats
Kemptville
Nova Scotia, BOW 1YO
*No Phone, Electronic Message Service*: 902 749 6553*

*Return calls are made only on Thursdays, and only absolutely necessary calls will be made collect. Usually your phone messages will be answered by mail.

Society has become over-crowded, over-protected and over-civilized. No one can live a fully human life without some experience of the wilderness.

In the Christian tradition, the desert, the mountain, the forest, and other solitary places are used synonymously to refer to the basic wilderness experience.

Nova Nada offers a unique environment for a wilderness retreat. It is located among majestic white pines, deep in the woods of Nova Scotia, overlooking a series of 3 freshwater lakes. In the summer, canoeing and swimming add adventure to your retreat; in winter, the snow and stillness give Nova Nada a special magic.

Men and women are welcome, young and old, married couples and singles, clergy and laypeople, Christians and practitioners of other spiritual traditions, and those without any religious affiliation. Length of stay depends on your particular needs—a week, a month, or a longer sabbatical—and the availability of a hermitage.

Each retreatant lives in a separate hermitage which contains a woodstove, basic cooking facilities, bed, desk, chair, food and linens. There is no electricity. Kerosene lamps provide warm light for reading.

A comfortable library, with a deck overhanging the lake, and a collection of over 3000 books including spiritual classics, the best contemporary literature, and an extensive tape library. Roam on paths scattered over 65 acres of quiet wilderness, 3 miles from the nearest neighbor.

One of the monks is available to help discern the spirit of your retreat. Community leaders are not available to retreatants. Structure is minimal: arrive Thursday, and on Friday morning one of the monks gives an orientation tour. Mass on Friday evening, followed by dinner with the community, which extends the Eucharist and offers an opportunity to get acquainted. Lively conversation at mealtimes.

On Saturday there are chores to prepare for the Sabbath—the highlight of the week. Benediction is on Saturday evening, followed by a vigil before the Blessed Sacrament throughout the night.

Sunday is a holy day of leisure beginning with Mass and breakfast together. The day is spent playing, praying and enjoying true Sabbath rest.

Monday and Tuesday are days of solitude with no scheduled communal activities. Wednesday begins with a quiet Mass, and is a work day for the monks. Each month there is an entire week of solitude when there are no communal activities, usually no retreats begin during these weeks.

Since manual labor is healthy and energizing, and a good preparation for prayer, retreatants are encouraged to participate in some such work.

Bring rugged, warm clothing year-round, a bathing suit in summer. You will need a battery-operated tape recorder and extra batteries if you intend to use the tape library. Be prepared to cook most of your meals in solitude. Simple food is provided.

Write requesting desired dates and an alternate date. A retreat application will be sent to you. Reservation is confirmed when you return this with your deposit. Arrive on Thursday, the regular town-trip day. Bring the confirmation card that will be sent to you. U.S. citizens will show this when crossing the border. Staff will meet you and return you to Yarmouth, a 40-mile drive. Only experienced 4-wheel drivers may drive into Nova Nada between December 1st and May 1st because of snow and mud on the unpaved road. Write for complete travel details and directions.

Suggested offerings:

CAN$44 per day, $290 per week; U.S.$40 per day, $265 per week. Couple may share a hermitage for and extra $15 per day. Ask about special rates for sabbaticals.

## TATAMAGOUCHE CENTRE
(Atlantic Christian Training Centre)
Rural Route #3
Tatamagouche, Nova Scotia BOK 1VO
☎ 902 657 2231
Contact: William Leslie, Administrative Co-Director

Operated by the United Church of Canada, the Tatamagouche Centre welcomes guests as space permits. Priority is given to programs and conferences.

Situated on 15 acres, the Centre overlooks the confluence of the French River and the Waugh River. The area is rich in the history of the Micmacs and Acadians. There are many outdoor activities and beaches.

65 people can be accommodated, shared occupancy, in 3 buildings. Campbell House, 19th century, has 10 bedrooms, 35 beds, private baths, and a lounge with fireplace. Creighton House is motel-like, 14 beds in 5 units, each with a second bedroom and private bath. The Lodge overlooks French River, 7 bedrooms, 17 beds each with bath, there are two shower/tubs in the building, lounge with fireplace, and kitchenettes.

Breakfast $4.50, Lunch $7.00, Supper $8.50, Snacks (3) $3.00. Meals are not always available at the Centre. But there are many restaurants in the village.

Overnight rate: $19 per person, $42 per person including meals as above.

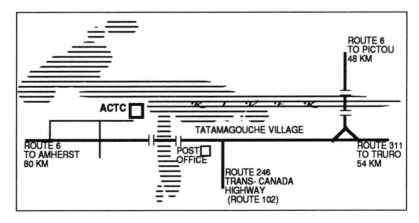

CRIEFF HILLS COMMUNITY
Presbyterian Church in Canada
Rural Route #2, Puslinch, Ontario NOB 2J0
(Near Guelph and Cambridge)
☎ 519 824 7898
FAX 519 824 7145
Contact: Manager

The property was first worked by Highland Scots. The Retreat Centre includes several historic houses and some modern buildings. It can accommodate individuals or up to 80 people. Outdoor activities include hiking on 250 acres of rolling countryside. There are wooded areas, a pond, and nature trails on the property.

The Hermitage is suitable for one person or a couple. It has a day bed with a trundle, a full bath and kitchenette. Rate: $22 per night single, $33 per night for a couple.

St. Andrew's House is suitable for 2-4 people. It includes 2 bedrooms, kitchen, full bathroom and a large living room. $40 per night minimum.

MADONNA HOUSE
Combermere, Ontario KOJ 1LO
☎ 613 756 3713
Contact: Registrar of Lay Men, Women or Priests

Madonna House is a lay apostolate composed of lay men, women, and priests—a family in the Roman Catholic Church, dedicated to loving and serving Christ in one another and in all men and women.

This Training Center is located in Combermere, Ontario, a small village about 200 miles northeast of Toronto, and about 125 miles west of Ottawa in the Madawaska Valley.

Of the approximately 200 members (staff and applicants) about 100 live in Combermere, where guests are also able to live and work with the community for varying lengths of time. The rest of the members serve in 22 field houses located in the U.S., Canada, West Indies, England, France, Brazil and Africa.

Catherine de Hueck Doherty, foundress of Madonna House, was born in Russia before the turn of the century, and grew up in a deeply Christian home with both Orthodox and Roman Catholic influences. She said that loneliness is the greatest poverty of our time. In each of the houses, the most important call is to form a community of love, to offer hospitality of the heart and home.

In 1952, in response to Pope Pius XII's suggestion, the young community voted to take promises of poverty, chastity and obedience. Catherine's life story has been told in the books *Tumbleweed* and *Cricket in My Heart* by her second husband, Eddie Doherty; in her autobiography *Fragments of My Life;* and in *Katia,* by Fr. Emile Briere—available through Madonna House Publications.

Life at Madonna House has a daily rhythm that is healing, wholesome—the inner clock starts to tick at a different rate from the harsh staccato of contemporary life. The sustaining rhythm of ordinary, simple life enables those who have come to Madonna House to become more aware of what exists within themselves, and in time they learn the great strength of Christian communal life.

At Madonna House, *Poustinia,* the Russian word meaning 'desert,' refers to a room or cabin, sparsely furnished, where one goes to pray and fast in silence and solitude for 24 hours. Members and long-term guests go to the poustinia with the permission of a spiritual director, determined by the work-needs of the community. In the poustinia, one may read the Bible and fast on bread and tea. In Combermere, the accent is on the

## Madonna House, Continued

community life, on the 'poustina of the heart,' that solitary place within each person where one meets God.

*Program For Guests:* Men and women in good health, usually aged 20 – 35, stay at Madonna House for varying lengths of time to share the life of a loving Christian family, practising the evangelical counsels of poverty, chastity and obedience, learning to incarnate the Gospel in the simple acts of every day, and listening, under spiritual direction, to the voice of the Lord in their lives.

People are asked to participate fully in the daily schedule of work, prayer and recreation, and to serve the poor in one another. We suggest spending at least a week here to best profit from the experience. No weekend guests.

*Cana Colony:* By the lake, a short distance from Madonna House, families renew their Christian life in a simple communal atmosphere. Each one-week session includes daily Mass in the rustic chapel, conferences and recreation. Several primitive cabins are available for families during the summer.

*Priests at Madonna House:* Several priests are permanent members of the Apostolate. Nearly half came as laymen and were ordained for the community. They live and work as part of the Madonna House family—celebrating the sacraments, teaching, praying and giving spiritual direction to members and guests. Priests from all over are welcome to participate in life here, with an accent on their needs.

*Pre-Seminarian Program and Associates:* 8 months of spiritual formation within the Madonna House community life.

*Madonna House Gift Shop:* Proceeds go directly to the poor. This is a special apostolate, staffed by Madonna House members chosen for this work. The shop is stocked entirely by donations, — antiques, gifts, clothing, handicrafts (some made at Madonna House), used books —ways of touching hearts and souls.

Call or write for further information.

---

### The Little Mandate
#### (The Spirit of Madonna House)

Arise – go! Sell all you possess... give it directly, personally to the poor. Take up My cross (their cross) and follow Me – going to the poor – being poor – being one with them – one with Me.

Little – be always little...simple – poor – childlike.

Preach the Gospel WITH YOUR LIFE – WITHOUT COMPROMISE –listen to the Spirit –He will lead you.

Do little things exceedingly well for love of Me.

Love – love – love, never counting the cost.

Go into the market place and stay with Me...pray...fast...pray always...fast.

Be hidden – be a light to your neighbor's feet. Go without fears into the depth of men's hearts... I shall be with you.

Pray always. I WILL BE YOUR REST

SISTERHOOD OF SAINT JOHN THE DIVINE
Saint John's Convent
1 Botham Road
Willowdale, Ontario M2N 2J5
☎ 416 266 2201 *or* 416 222 4442 *(Guest Wing)*
Contact: Guest Sister

The Sisterhood of St. John offers Private Retreats and Formal Retreats with some spiritual direction. The Guesthouse facilities are for those seeking a place of quiet, rest, reflection and prayer; and also for Group Retreats and Conducted Retreats. A Schedule is available on request.

1994 Rates: $40 overnight, with meals. Group rates or Conducted Retreats, a little more.

Holiday visitors are welcome in summer, those wishing to combine a quiet place with some sightseeing of Toronto and surrounding area: $25 per night, including breakfast. Lunch and supper: $7.50 each.

The Sisterhood of St. John the Divine was founded in Toronto in 1884 as a monastic community for women, committed to a life of prayer and service within the Anglican Church of Canada. These women are from a variety of Christian traditions, ethnic and national backgrounds.

St. John's Convent is the Motherhouse of the community where novices are trained, an infirmary provides nursing care for the Sisters as required, and retreats, workshops, and quiet days are conducted. Some of the Sisters preach outside the convent. A major part of their ministry involves the large, active Guest Wing.

The ministry of hospitality, whereby the sisters share their life of community and prayer with guests, is for men and women and families. Guests are invited to join in the daily traditional Offices of the Church—Morning Prayer, Noonday Intercessions, Evening Prayer, and Compline, in addition to a daily celebration of the Eucharist.

SAINT JOSEPH'S CENTRE OF SPIRITUALITY
Box 155, Station A
Hamilton, Ontario L8N 3A2
☎ 905 528 0138
FAX 905 528 8883
Contact: The Secretary, Mon-Fri. 8:45-4:30

*Mission Statement:*

St. Joseph's Centre of Spirituality is sponsored by The Sisters of St. Joseph of Hamilton and, since its opening in 1983, has been located in the four-storey West wing of their Motherhouse. Thus the Centre's mission and goals are rooted in the Mission of the Sisters: *To heal broken relationships, to reconcile and unite people with one another and with God.* Staff at the Centre strive to be instruments of this unity and reconciliation.

We offer organized programs which provide a wide range of growth opportunities and spiritual enrichment. We are committed to the creation of an atmosphere of hospitality where people can meet their Divine Teacher and Healer.

We strive to empower groups and individuals to discover and tap the riches within themselves and thereby improve their own lives and move all creation to greater harmony.

Any group whose objectives conforms with our Mission Statement, is welcome to rent facilities for a day or overnight.

The Centre staff can arrange private retreats of one day or more, with or without a director.

Spiritual Accompaniment is available.

The Centre has spacious grounds, 33 single bedrooms, a chapel, dining-room for 72, meeting rooms and conference rooms. It is a smoke-free environment.

Call or write for complete details and a program schedule.

SISTERS OF THE GOOD SHEPHERD
Regina Mundi
R.R. # 2
19309 5th Concession Road
Queensville Ontario LOG 1RO
Contact: Sister Florence McCadden RGS

The Sisters of The Good Shepherd provide for Group Retreats, Private Retreats, and welcome visitors.

Peace Cottage accommodates 2 people, with one bedroom, bath, kitchen and lounge. There is also a pool. Prepare your own meals.

Call or write for further information.

CENTER FOR SPIRITUAL DEVELOPMENT
Sisters of St. Martha
Mount St. Mary's
141 Mount Edward Road
Sherwood, Prince Edward Island C1A 7M8
☎ 902 892 6585
Contact: Sr. Marie Cahill or Sr. Edna Gallant

The Center for Spiritual Development is a Retreat Center located within the Motherhouse –Mount St. Mary's. It offers Weekend Retreats, Workshops, and Reflection Days.

Christian Meditation on Tuesday mornings 10-11AM, and Tuesday evenings, 7:30–8:30PM. A teaching is included in the hour.

Spiritual Direction is available for anyone who wishes to be accompanied in his or her Christian life. The journey always begins where you are.

Focusing—a Bio-Spirituality which teaches interconnectedness with what the mind thinks and the body experiences—is offered in a group or 1:1 setting.

Praying with Scripture—a reflection on the Word of God and our own experience. This learning can be done individually or in small groups.

Call or write for current program and further information.

*MARTHA'S SPINDLE is a symbol of the transforming power of Jesus Christ in our lives. The Spindle represents CONVERSION, and is at the same time an instrument of change.*

LA MAISON DU RENOUVEAU
870 Carre de Tracy Est
C.P. 7127
Charlesbourg, Quebec G1G 5E1
☎ 418 623 5597
Contact: Director

La Maison de Renouveau is a Renewal Centre for groups, private retreats, and days of recollection. Evening programs are provided too. With advance notice, the staff can organize and conduct retreat offerings, conferences and workshops. Meals can be provided by a professional chef as needed.

55 people can be accommodated overnight, in an atmosphere of simplicity and calm. The rooms are comfortable and tastefully decorated. There is a chapel, library, spacious dining room, conference room, smaller meeting rooms, and a bookstore.

The house lends itself equally well to groups and to those who seek a place of silence and prayer. It enjoys the tranquility of the country, with plenty of trees and lawn—a hilltop setting with a wonderful view of surrounding areas, yet it is only 15 minutes to midtown Quebec. Also, 25 minutes away is the Sanctuary of Sainte—Anne de Beaupre, a marvelous place of pilgrimage in North America. [See page 214].

The Centre is operated by the Secular Institute of Pius X, whose evangelization work includes the publication of The Editions of Renewal and the Magazine I Believe. Both can be ordered from the following address: 1645 80 Rue Est, C.P. 7605, Charlesbourg, QC, Canada GIG 5W6. Phone: 418 628 3445.

For further information, and to make reservations, phone or write La Maison de Renouveau.

MONASTERE DU CARMEL
4705 Avenue Tewkesbury
Tewkesbury, CTE Quebec GOA 4PO

Women and married couples are welcome to experience a Private Retreat at Monastere du Carmel. A letter of recommendation from a parish priest, minister, or other person in ministry is required.

Facilities include a small, 5-room guest house in a marvelous setting in the mountains. The atmosphere is quiet and peaceful. The nuns are French-speaking most of the time.

The monastery is 40 km. from the city.

Write in advance for reservations.

SAINTE ANNE DE BEAUPRE BASILICA SHRINE
Quebec GOA 3CO
☎ 418 827 3781
FAX 418 827 4530
Contact: The Secretariat of the Basilica

Basilica Inn
P.O. Box 57
Sainte Anne de Beaupre, Quebec GOA 3CO
☎ 418 827 4475
FAX 418 827 5162

The Inn faces the Basilica. It has 107 rooms with shower and toilet, a cafeteria, roomy lounge, chapel and elevator. Fire-proof building. Single beds in each room.

Rates: Single: $35/day; Double: $40; Triple: $46. Call or write for reservations.

There are many hotels, inns and motels in the area. A list can be obtained when writing to the Shrine for further information.

The Basilica is a great masterpiece of architecture. While on pilgrimage, it is asked that you maintain a respectful silence, and that proper, dignified dress be worn.

Hostesses and guides are at your service from May to mid-October. The information center is open year-round. Aides of St. Anne can assist wheelchair users. The elevator in the vestibule of the Basilica is wheelchair accessible.

Camping on the shore is free for pilgrims, from June 24th to early September.

There is a projection room at the Shrine, video tapes, picnic tables, restrooms, Sunday recitals from 3–4PM.

*Cyclorama* –the world's largest Panorama, on exhibit since 1895, was created by Paul Philippoteaux, the celebrated panoramist from Paris, and his 5 assistants. Executed in Munich from 1878–1882, the monumental work is 14 metres high and 110 metres in circumference: 1,540 square metres of amazing illusion. Unique in Canada and the world, considering its subject –the City of Jerusalem and environs 'On the very day of the Crucifixion.'

In the Basilica car park is a wax museum. 20 waxwork tableaux tell the story of St. Anne and the history of the Shrine at Beaupre.

*Saint Anne De Beaupre Basilica, Continued*

The Shrine, dedicated to the honor of the grandmother of Christ, is one of the oldest pilgrimage centres in North America. For more than 300 years, pilgrims have been coming to St. Anne de Beaupre from almost everywhere in search of a stronger faith life and, often, in the hope of relief from their moral or physical afflictions.

A priest is available for private consultations between 8:30 and 5PM.

An information brochure is printed in several languages. Summer hours are 8:30 to 9PM. June 6th is the official opening of the pilgrimage season. Write or call for particulars of devotions and Shrine activities and schedules –daily Masses, Adoration and Prayers for the Sick, Rosary, Stations of the Cross, Candlelight Procession.

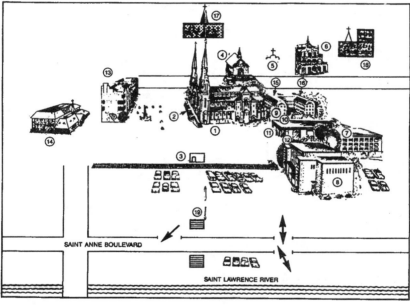

1. *Basilica*
2. *Information Office*
3. *Reception Booth*
4. *Memorial Chapel and Fountain*
5. *Hillside Stations of the Cross*
6. *Holy Stairs*
7. *Annals Office*
8. *Historial and Basilica Museum*
9. *Church Store*
10. *Blessings Office*

11. *Restrooms*
12. *Lunch Tables*
13. *Saint Anne's Hospital*
14. *Basilica Inn*
15. *Redemptorists' Monastery*
16. *Saint Alphonsus Seminary*
17. *Redemptoristines' Convent*
18. *Franciscan Nuns' Convent*
19. *Underground Passage*

## QUEEN'S HOUSE RETREAT AND RENEWAL CENTRE
601 Taylor Street West
Saskatoon, Saskatchewan S7M 0C9
☎ 306 242 1916
FAX 306 653 5941
Contact: Program Director

Queen's House offers Group Retreats and Workshops for Spiritual and Personal Growth. – Directed Retreats – Spiritual Direction – Private Retreats.

Call or write for further information.

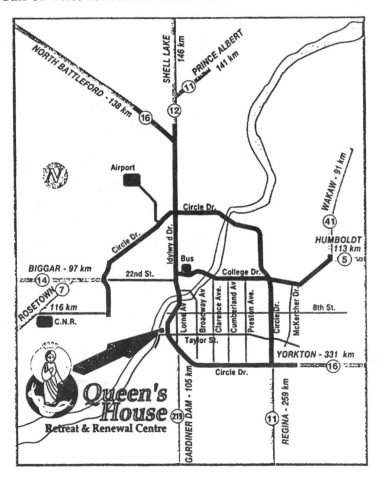

URSULINE SISTERS
Box 89
Bruno, Saskatchewan SOK OSO
☎ 306 369 2993
Contact: Guestsister

The Ursuline Sisters offer a quiet time to relax and pray for Retreats, Groups, Workshops and Meetings.

Most rooms are dormitory-style with private cubicles, baths and showers in central rooms.

Closed July and August.

Rates: $7.50 per night; Meals: Breakfast, $2.75, Lunch $6, Dinner $6.

Call or write for further information.

URSULINE HOUSE OF PROVIDENCE
755 3rd Northwest
Swift Current, Saskatchewan S9H OT2

No formal retreats. The House is open to those who want a place for a few hours, a day, or a weekend of quiet time and reflection.

Write for complete details.

PRAIRIE CHRISTIAN TRAINING CENTRE
P.O. Box 159
Fort Qu'Appelle, Saskatchewan  SOG 1S0
☎ 306 332 5691
Contact: Chris McNaughton, Administrative Secretary

Operated by the United Church of Canada, the Prairie Christian Training Center offers Private and Group Retreats for short-term stays. A variety of Continuing Education Courses are also provided for lay people and ministers.

Facilities include accommodations for up to 50 people in double rooms. There is a bookshop featuring spiritual and ministerial resources, and Third World craftwork.

The Centre is situated in the rural Qu'Appelle Valley near Echo Lake and the town of Fort Qu'Appelle.

Call or write ahead for complete details and to make reservations.

*All nature speaks to me of God.*

# HOUSES OF PRAYER
# & RETREAT CENTERS
# IN OTHER COUNTRIES

# ABADIA SANTA MARIA DE GUADALUPE
Hermana Hospedera
MI–090
62300
Ahuatepec, Morelos
☎ & FAX 52 73 820208

This *Hospedera* is a place of rest for those seeking peace, for those seeking God. People may come on an individual or a group basis (up to 20) for a Private Personal Retreat, for Solitude and Meditation, or for a collective Formal Retreat. Guests are invited to share the liturgical prayer in the chapel with the monastic community (Mass and chanting of the Psalms).

*Accommodations:* Individual rooms, with private or shared bathroom, are provided, as well as 3 meals a day, at specific hours.

The current daily rate is U.S.$25 per person, 3 meals included. This rate may vary with inflation and the exchange rate. However, in case of difficulty an arrangement could be made so that the financial does not hinder the spiritual element.

For making arrangements, people desiring to spend time at Abadia Santa Maria de Guadalupe should be able to communicate in Spanish or French. The nuns do not speak English.

Reservations should be made preferably two months in advance if coming from abroad. A 25% deposit should be sent in advance, at the time of reservation.

The monastery is located in Ahuatepec, a small town in the outskirts of the city of Cuernavaca, approximately 50 miles from Mexico City by a 4-lane toll-road.

## CUERNAVACA RETREAT CENTER
Benedictine Sisters
Retreat Hospitality Experience

*Write To:*
Benedictine Monks
Weston Priory
58 Priory Hill Road
Weston VT 05161
U.S.A.
☎ 802 824 5409

The monks of Weston Priory arrange groups travelling to Mexico for this non–traditional retreat experience, and also an unusual pilgrimage to the Shrine of Guadalupe. Sisters take you on tour each day, and you will see how the real Mexico lives.

16 people can be accommodated at a time. Rate: U.S.$35 per day for 10 days, this includes meals, room and board; travel on land in Mexico is an additional U.S.$50. Send a deposit of U.S.$100 to Weston Priory when you have contacted them about the availability of space for this retreat experience.

You will need a tourist card from the airline and U.S. citizens need proof of citizenship (passport, birth certificate with raised seal and photo I.D.) [Citizens of other countries may need to enquire of a travel agent about documentation].

December 12th is the Feast of Our Lady of Guadalupe.

If you are organizing a group of 6 or more, 2 tuition scholarships are available, valued at U.S.$350 each.

The Sisters are very hospitable, accommodations are modest but comfortable, and food is home cooked and very good.

## SAINT MARGARET'S CONVENT
Box 857
Port-Au-Prince

*Mailing Address:*
Saint Margaret's Convent Paul'
Agape Flats, 7990 15th Street East
Sarasota FL 34243
U.S.A.
Contact: Sister Marie Margaret

St. Margaret's Convent offers Private Retreats in the mountains at the 4500 foot level, above the sea at Kenscoff, for one or several days. Beautiful scenery, cool weather –pack a sweater.

Hike to the *Wynne's Farm*, guided by Janie Wynne, daughter of the 96 year-old man who created 'Mr. Wynne's Garden,' a life-long project to make Haiti more productive of food, producing rare fruits and plants of all sorts from all parts of the world. Mr. Wynne came to Haiti aged 23, from upstate New York, married a Haitian, and climbed the mountain daily until the age of 92. The climb is steep and rocky and takes about 1 1/2 hours. When the farm was started there was only one eucalyptus tree. Now there is a pine forest, and many food-bearing trees and plants.

As you climb further over heavy grass, you come to the open rain-fed reservoir, the source of water for plants on the top of the mountain, 6000+ feet above sea-level. The view from this vantage is a very beautiful grouping of mountains, dotted with small houses and villages.

Janie Wynne's dream is to continue this extraordinary project, to be used as a teaching farm or national park, where young people can learn about the variety and care of God's green Earth on this unique and lonely mountain.

Sister recommends this hike to those who are capable, and interested in seeing what one man's efforts and dream can produce. Janie gives a wonderful ecological talk on her tour of the farm and mountain. Individuals and groups can write to St. Margaret's Convent if they are interested in having Janie guide them on this special mountain project.

At present Sister Marie Margaret will be glad to acknowledge your enquiries, but retreats and hikes/tours of 'Mr. Wynne's Garden' cannot be accommodated until the political climate in Haiti is normalized. Please write for further information.

MOUNT OF PRAYER
Monastery of Benedictine Nuns
P.O. Box 778
Castries, Saint Lucia, West Indies
☎ 809 45 21282 *or* 31533
FAX 809 45 27845
Contact: Mother Marianna Pinto OSB

The Monastery is a school, a workshop, a home, the Gate of Heaven. The Benedictine nuns come to the monastery to seek God according to the means indicated by St. Benedict for daily monastic living: The Divine Office, Sacred Reading, intellectual and manual work, The Nun is not merely in the Monastery to gain qualifications but to reach the full maturity of Christian life, and takes vows of Obedience, Conversion of Manners, and Stability.

Work is shared by all, according to each one's abilities. This work is not merely a pastime, it is creative and by it the community earns its living. In the monastic life no one is asked to forego her natural gifts, but is expected to use them in God's service. Often, quite unsuspected talents are discovered and developed. In the Monastery there is a variety of activities: handicraft, baking altar-breads, artistic work such as making vestments and banners, beekeeping, typesetting and layout of the *Catholic Chronicle*.

The Nuns are also engaged in various apostolic works such as: counseling, giving and providing a place for retreats, spiritual guidance, and different forms of hospitality.

Hospitality is like a sacrament for the Nuns –it is a bridge linking them to the world. The Nuns hear the call made by a needy world, and the world hears the response made by the nuns.

Call or write for further information regarding retreats, spiritual guidance, monastic life, and hospitality in their guest house.

CORPUS CHRISTI CARMELITES
Mount Carmel Novitiate
Tunapuna, Trinidad, West Indies
Contact: Sister Ann Parker O. CARM.

We accept visitors on a short stay basis, and some come for retreats or quiet periods of reflection.

The Convent is comprised of the Generalate and Novitiate. It is beautifully situated on the Northern Range, but is only 7 miles from the airport and quite accessible. The lifestyle at the Convent is simple and quiet. Visitors share our accommodation and facilities. As we do not have separate accommodation, we are unable to accept married couples or men.

Please write for further information.

WILLOWBANK
P.O. Box MA 296
Sandy MA BX, Bermuda
☎ 809 234 1616
FAX 809 234 3373
Contact: Reservations
*For Reservations only,* call toll-free in the U.S. 800-752-8493
and in Canada: 800 463 8444

Willowbank is a small, family-style resort hotel, comparable to the most popular hotels in Bermuda, but at more affordable rates. It is sponsored by the Willowbank Foundation —a non-denominational Christian Trust.

For 30 years, this unique place has taken care of the spirit as well as the body, eliminating TV's and phones from rooms to encourage fellowship, rest, recreation and renewal. Willowbank provides a caring Christian atmosphere in a family setting.

The phone in the office/lobby area may be used. Also, postcards, stamps, and a delightful book telling the Willowbank story, are available at the service desk.

Willowbank is set in over 6 acres of semi-tropical gardens on a promontory overlooking Ely's Harbour and the Atlantic Ocean —a location of great natural beauty with dramatic views, cliffs, beaches and sunsets. In particular, the dining room overlooks the ocean and provides opportunity to experience magnificent sunsets as one dines by large bay windows.

The original two-centuries old Bermuda homestead with its traditional tray ceilings and old Bermuda cedar beams, is the heart of the estate, complemented by modern guest accommodations —single story units in clusters of 3 to 14 rooms.

Rooms are pleasant and air-conditioned. There is a spacious dining room, patio, sitting and meeting rooms, and a cozy library. Family style main meals are served at one sitting, announced by the ringing of the ancient ship's bell, and grace is said before each meal. Most meals are in the dining room, but there is an outside barbecue, weather permitting, about twice a week. Dress code for dinner only. Lunch is available in the coffee shop at extra cost. Afternoon tea in the library.

Activities include: Fun-nights, devotional programs, 2 all-weather tennis courts, shuffleboard, and a sheltered temperature-controlled freshwater swimming pool. There are two white sandy beaches and a dock off the rocky headland where guests sometimes feed the tropical fish.

The climate is temperate. There are 2 seasons, no rainy season —summer temperatures prevail from May to mid-November. Hurricanes are more a legend than an experience. The atmosphere of Bermuda is one of British reserve and dignified informality. Dress is conservative.

Send for the current rate schedule, including the special incentive package for the popular off-season. A deposit is required with reservations. No credit cards or personal checks. Rates include breakfast, dinner, afternoon tea, —no gratuities. There is a 6% government tax, except with some of the incentive packages.

Transportation to and from the airport can be arranged by Willowbank with advance notice. Approximate cost for a taxi is $33, including baggage handling.

Passes are available for unlimited use of bus and ferry for 3 or 7 days. Mopeds and taxis are other means for guests to get around the islands. There are no car rentals in Bermuda.

Write for complete information about Willowbank and general information about Bermuda.

*That men in a hurried and anxious world might find rest, recreation and renewed purpose.*

# A PILGRIM'S BOOKLIST

**A Grief Observed**
C.S. Lewis                          Bantam, 1963

**A Memory for Wonders**
Mother Veronica LeGoulard          Ignatius Press, 1993

**A Place Apart**
Basil Pennington                    Doubleday, 1983

**Carmelite Meditations: God Alone and I**
                                    St. Teresa's Press, 1965

**Centering Prayer**
Basil Pennington                    Doubleday, 1982

**Christian Vision, The**
John Powell                         Tabor TMP, 1984

**Daily We Touch Him**
Basil Pennington                    Doubleday, 1977

**Early Will I Seek You**
David Hazard                        Bethany House, 1991

**Getting The Most From Your Retreat**
Katherine Doyle                     St. Anthony Messenger, 1990

**Gift From The Sea: Selections**
Anne Lindbergh                      Hallmark, 1967

**Greatest Story Ever Told**
Fulton Oursler                      Doubleday, 1949

**I Have Found God:** *Elizabeth of The Trinity*
Trans. Sr. Aletheia Kane           ICS Pub., 1993

**Imitation of Christ:** *Thomas Á Kempis*
Trans. Robert Dudley                ACB/Source 1980
**Joshua**
Joseph Girzone                      Doubleday, 1994

**Little Flowers of St. Francis**
Trans. Abby Alger                    Peter Pauper Press, 1964

**My Russian Yesterdays**
Catherine de Hueck Doherty           Madonna House, 1990

**No Man Is An Island**
Thomas Merton                        HBJ, 1955

**Permission To Be**
Eric Blakebrough                     Daybreak/DLT, 1992

**Preferring Christ:** *Devotional Commentary on the Rule of St. Benedict*
Norvene Vest                         Source Books, 1990

**The Rule of St. Benedict: RB1980**
                                     Liturgical Press, 1981

**Self-Portrait In Letters** *–Edith Stein Vol V,*
Trans. Josephine Koeppel             ICS Pub., 1993

**Seven Storey Mountain, The**
Thomas Merton                        HBJ, 1978

**Spiritual Exercise of St. Ignatius Loyola**
Trans. Thomas Corbishley             ACB/Source 1973

**Story of A Soul:** *St. Thérèse of Lisieux*
Trans. John Clarke                   ICS Pub., 1976

**Strange Gods Before Me**
Mother Mary Francis                  Franciscan Herald Press, 1976

**Thoughts In Solitude**
Thomas Merton                        Shambhala Pub., 1993

**Voices of Silence:** *Lives of the Trappists Today*
Frank Bianco                         Paragon House, 1991

**Way of the Heart, The**
Henri Nouwen                         Ballantine, 1981

# INDEX

# INDEX